# Footprints of Faith

### stories of YWAM in South Asia

## Sonya Svoboda

YWAM
PUBLISHING

# Footprints of Faith

## stories of YWAM in South Asia

## Sonya Svoboda

**Footprints of Faith**
Stories of YWAM in South Asia

Copyright © 2006 by Sonya Svoboda
ALL RIGHTS RESERVED

ISBN-10: 81-89554-02-6
ISBN-13: 978-81-89554-02-6

Published by :
YWAM Publishing
Chennai, India

Design & Layout :
Shini & Rob Abraham
YWAM International Communications, Colorado Springs, CO, USA

Printed in India
For Worldwide Distribution

For additional copies of this book, please contact the publisher:
YWAM Publishing
No. 7 East Spurtank Road • Chetput
Chennai • Tamil Nadu • India 600016
Email tks61@yahoo.com

# My Litany of Thanks

I f I had to state just one lesson I've learned while writing this book it would be this: that writing is not a solitary task. Many have stood around me, lending their talents to the manuscript as well as their support. This book would not be what it is without each one of them.

My first thanks goes to the leaders of YWAM South Asia for entrusting me with this project. Many of you have known me since I only came up to your waist!!! Yet you were willing to let me write this and didn't wait to find someone older and wiser!

When I listed the people I would need to contact, I wondered how I would finish them all as I had to coordinate around their schedules as well as mine. But many of you graciously gave up your time to let me ask you questions upon questions. Thank you for recalling and retelling events which happened over 20 years ago. Thank you for putting up with my persistent questioning and patiently responding to my numerous emails and phone calls. Although I wasn't able to use every interview (as much as I would have liked to), each story I heard deposited something in my own heart and gave me a truer picture of the passion each of you has for Jesus! Thank you for being faithful over these past years to the call of God upon your lives.

In February 2004, I attended an Authors' Training School in Kona, Hawaii. I went with the vaguest idea of the book's theme and was told by many that, out of all the students, I had the most complicated project. But at the end I emerged with a solid theme and knew exactly how it was going to be executed. This is due to the wonderful staff who questioned what I was doing, picked me up and put me back on the right road. A special thanks goes to Twink DeWitt who mercilessly but lovingly edited my chapters early on and infected me with her own enthusiasm about the book.

To all those who blessed me with their prayer covering, thank you! I felt your prayers at each step. There were many times I felt like giving up and wondered if I was doing the right thing. I can't count the number of times I felt inadequate for this job. But at the back of my mind was a sense of purpose that would not let me give up. Despite all the discouragement I've walked through in the past months, I knew I would complete this job and be satisfied with the results. I believe it was your prayers that were the quiet encouragement at the back of my mind. Thank you! You contributed more to the book than you know.

A special thanks to my Aunt Kris Meidal for initiating this book. Your interviews were a lifesaver and played a large role in shaping the framework. As a fellow-writer your words of advice, love, and encouragement kept my head up throughout the frustrating hours of feeling like I was going nowhere.

To Scott and Sandi Tompkins, my editors: You have done a marvelous job at chipping off the bumps in my manuscript. You both have been a constant source of encouragement, always telling me the end was near. I thank God for both of you. You came at a time when I wasn't sure what lay ahead. You have truly understood the heart of what I want to communicate and have been faithful to the task of clarifying this message. May God bless you both many times for this extraordinary labor of love.

To my family: There are not enough words to sum up all you mean to me and your tremendous support during the writing of this book. Dad, you've lent your time beyond anything I ever asked for. You pointed out my areas of strength and weakness. You taught me how to see the bigger picture. In the midst of emails to answer, meetings to attend, and papers to write for your doctorate, you gave up your time to assist me during the interviews, asking questions I hadn't even thought about but which opened up a whole new window. Beyond that, you read through each chapter, catching little but significant issues I hadn't seen. You saw the bigger picture when I couldn't even see past the chapter I was currently working on. Mom, you've been a tremendous pillar of support for me during this time. You kept encouraging me through my tears and gave me the courage to continue. Your prayers, emails, and phone calls were very special to me during this time. You kept gently prodding me on, and your faith in me has held me up throughout many of the difficult times. Thanks for answering my many questions regarding minor details, and catching important discrepancies in all of my drafts. I couldn't have completed this book without the two of you and might have lost my sanity. Paul, thank you for putting up with my countless hours of writing even when you wanted me to do something with you. Thank you also for making me relax with our many games of ping-pong and Prince of Persia. You're a wonderful brother! Ana, I have many memories from the beginning days in Chennai, ones of growing up, and I'm glad I was able to share those with you. Thank you for being a wonderful sister.

To my precious Lord and Savior: Without You this book would cease to exist. Just as You were the One who sustained my parents and many others in YWAM South Asia, so have You sustained me with Your grace throughout this writing journey. Without You, all this would have been impossible.

~ Sonya Svoboda

# FOREWORD

*You are holding in your hands a firsthand account of a work of the Holy Spirit in the lives of ordinary people who believe in an extraordinary God. Having been involved both as a participant and an observer from the early days of YWAM's beginning in South Asia, I can with great confidence say with the psalmist, "this is the Lord's doing, and it is marvelous in our eyes" (Ps. 118:23).*

*Author Sonya Svoboda's parents and the other prominent characters in "Footprints of Faith" began their entrance into my life as co-workers and friends. They have now become my heroes. The sacrifices they made and the years of laboring in love have now produced eternal fruit in that vast Garden of God that is the Indian subcontinent.*

*I was thrilled when asked to write the foreword for Sonya's new book. Having known "up-close and personal" the key players involved, it gave me occasion for some happy reflection on those early days.*

*There was Kalafi Moala, barely 30 himself, who captivated our young hearts with fiery passion and a vision that the "mullions" (Kalafi's rendering of millions!) of lost people in South Asia could be reached. His apostolic faith and vision were contagious.*

*From the early prayer meetings and commissioning times in the "Tin Cathedral" at the Honolulu base and the early conferences at Mahabalipuram in Tamil Nadu, Kalafi's vision took root. My wife Linda and I had recently arrived at the Honolulu base from Fiji with a baby and no money! There we met Steve Cochrane, a skinny kid from Seattle who took the challenge for Calcutta, along with Brad Carr who had impressed me with his humility as my DTS outreach leader. There was Lis [Elisabeth Baumann], barely 20, who heard the Lord speak to her about Nepal, and along with Judy became our "team of two" to the Himalayan region. Later came Leaula, a fun-loving Islander who kept us entertained with Samoan "slap-dances" and an appetite that would consume anything edible. These ordinary people and others became the catalysts for God's dreams for South Asia.*

*In January of 1983 Kalafi and wife Leda took off to pioneer our new work in Japan and left Linda and I in charge of the still fledgling work in Honolulu.*

8   ❧

*We were running the base, as well as the School of Evangelism, and we quickly became over-extended. We prayed for reinforcements and it was then that Tim and Karol Svoboda landed in Hawaii from Urbana [Illinois, USA]. They agreed to assume leadership of the SOE allowing me to be free to travel and recruit.*

*Shortly thereafter, Tim and Karol informed us that God was calling them to Madras. We were thrilled at the prospect of another team going to India, but sad to lose leadership needed on the home front, not to mention the fact that we would have to say goodbye to our new friends. As they say, the rest is history. History of a glorious work of God in ordinary people that I'm sure will captivate you as you read.*

*It has been my privilege to observe God's hand on these spiritual warriors firsthand, and to also hear of the growth in the second and third generation of pioneers who are busy serving Jesus in the subcontinent and beyond.*

*"It is the Lord's doing, and He is marvelous in our eyes."*

*Danny Lehmann*
*Honolulu, Hawaii 2005*

# TABLE OF CONTENTS

❧

# PROLOGUE
# Tracing Backwards

I fingered the silver bangles on my arms, delighting in the tinkling sound they made whenever I moved. Little mirrors on my *salwar*[1] caught the shine of the sun, and I pushed my blue and gold *dupatta* scarf back on my shoulder for the hundredth time.

Usually I wore the typical college student uniform — jeans and a t-shirt — but not today. This morning I stopped playing the all-American girl role that I felt so ill-fitted for. Everything I was wearing today shouted out who I am on the inside, the part of me you can't see. It was World Culture Day, an annual celebration at Eastern University in Pennsylvania, where I was a student. This day was set apart to celebrate the various cultures represented on the campus.

Surrounding me behind a display table were other Indians, ready to answer questions about India. Everyone understood why *they* were there. But when they saw me, some asked, "Why are *you* here?"

I explained that I grew up in India. And like today, I am part of the white minority. I had become comfortable in that status. To now be part of the American majority marked a difficult cultural shift for me. I teetered between these two worlds, and sometimes my life in India seemed like someone else's story. On those days I wondered if it was here among America's many white faces that I actually belonged.

But the feeling in my heart and the stamps in my passports defined my true identity. Since 1983 Chennai (formerly Madras), India, had been home for me. In January of that year, my parents led a 17-member School of Evangelism (SOE) team to Kuala Lumpur, Malaysia on a 20-plus hour flight from Honolulu. Three months later our family was on our long-awaited flight to India. My parents had invited the SOE team members to join us, but with the warning we had no plans to leave India. Nine members from the team followed my parents, myself (almost 3 years old), and my 15-month-old sister Ana to Kolkata (formerly Calcutta). After spending three weeks there, we settled in Chennai. Two remained in Kolkata, and five came down with us. This bustling south Indian port city of Chennai became the centre of my young life.

That was not my parents' first trip to India. In 1975, they had driven overland from Lausanne, Switzerland, as part of a Youth With A Mission (YWAM) School of Evangelism (SOE) outreach. Then they were both single, in their early twenties. In 1983 they returned as a missionary family sent out by the YWAM Honolulu base.

Although YWAM was founded in 1960, it was just getting established in South Asia when my family arrived. Honolulu proved to be a strategic location for carrying out YWAM's vision for releasing young people into missions. It was at the Honolulu base that Steve Cochrane, Elisabeth (Baumann) Cochrane, Brad Carr, David Paul and my parents were motivated to step out in faith and pioneer YWAM South Asia.

Danny Lehmann, the Honolulu base leader, is a surfer-turned-evangelist whose passion for missions is legendary. His zeal for helping young people "to know God and make Him known" (YWAM's motto) has carried countless teams, both long and short-term, into South Asia throughout the years.

Danny's zeal was fuelled by Kalafi Moala, a Tongan YWAMer who founded the Honolulu base with the dream of using it a springboard for missions into Asia. This vision is still the main focus of YWAM Honolulu today. Kalafi carried out his vision with selfless abandon in the 1980s. Many of those who pioneered YWAM South Asia look back to their years in Honolulu as a critical time of formation. They credit Danny and Kalafi as their key mentors and a determining factor in the existence of YWAM South Asia today.

While Danny's passion and Kalafi's boundless faith in their call to missions launched these young people into Asia, it was truly the grace of God that kept them in India, Nepal and Bangladesh through many hardships.

Despite those difficulties, the last 23 years have passed all too quickly for the early pioneers of YWAM South Asia. Of the original 21, nine remain there today. Their lives are seamlessly connected to the work there, their roots deep in the soil of these nations. In informal gatherings with them, there is abundant laughter over the stories of mistakes and successes in their ministry through the years. But these times often end with a humbling awe of the miracles God has accomplished through the years, and the realization that nothing was accomplished without God.

From a humble beginning of those 21 people and three bases (Chennai, Kolkata and Kathmandu) in 1983, YWAM's work in South Asia has grown to now touch 100+ cities and includes over 1,000 staff, who have trained 10,000 students through their Discipleship Training Schools. My father became the first National Director of YWAM India in 1989, and his vision for seeing Indian nationals leading the mission was fulfilled six years later when Sam Dharam succeeded him. Sam decentralized the mission's structure, sparking further growth and innovation. In the early days the staff was mostly made up of foreigners, but today the ratio of national workers far outweighs the foreign staff.

As I grew up and traveled around the world, I began to see a different side of my YWAM roots. As a child, it was normal for me to see God at work, to hear of miracles, to have five or even more countries represented in my living room, to go on our knees to ask God for a few *rupees*. That was the lifestyle of most YWAM India leaders I knew. So when I would travel abroad and hear people speak about my parents, the Cochranes, the Pauls, and other pioneers with such awe and respect, I began to realize the importance of this work I grew up with and so often took for granted.

My memories of the pioneers are like any other child's memory of their parents' friends. I remember my sister Ana and I looking forward to Steve Cochrane's visits because he would entertain us with his "beaver faces." I remember when Wendy Mahbert (now Paul) dressed up as a clown to surprise the kids at my sister's birthday party. I remember meals shared with all kinds of interesting people. I know my parents' memories are far different from mine. They saw the big picture of events that were changing the entire spiritual climate of a nation. I often probed for their stories and each one gave me more insight into God's heart for me and the people of India.

In September 2003, I was honored to be asked to write YWAM South Asia's history. I accepted because I knew there was a message God wanted to communicate through these stories. I am now the same age (25) as most of the pioneers were in 1983. When I try to think of myself doing what they did, I am overcome with self-doubt. But I know many of them had similar doubts when the opportunity opened before them. As I submerge myself deeper into this writing process, I see parallels between this writing journey and the journey of those YWAM South Asia pioneers. It is a large task, and I am only able to complete it with God's help and guidance at every corner. While I wrote this book, I couldn't escape into my childlike notion of the normalcy of our work in India. I had to keep the large picture in front of me constantly, and I found myself sending up numerous prayers of thanks while I wrote.

In May 2003, I graduated from college. As a gift, my mother put together a scrapbook for me. The pictures in it depicted different stages of my life. A few days after graduation, I sat at a table sharing this book with my friends. My mother stood behind my chair as I flipped through the pages. She stopped me at a photo taken on my last visit home. The photo was from a small gathering for some of the YWAM workers who had been together since the 1980s. We were from various parts of India, as well as other countries. Pointing to the picture, my mother said, "Those are the girls' aunties and uncles."

I knew some might wonder how people who bear no physical resemblance to us could be called family. True, those aunties and uncles weren't my blood relatives, but they were the closest family I had at the time. Now that I am an adult, I see how blessed I was to have them as family. Through my research I have come to understand what their commitment and sacrifice meant. These aunties and uncles, who seemed so ordinary to me, risked everything they had to bring hope and salvation to the more than one billion people of South Asia.

1

# Spying Out the Land

*After 26 hours of being jostled and rocked about, I eased off the Coromandel Express, grateful to finally be in Kolkata. Twenty years earlier, my family and others arrived here with little more than their conviction that God was calling them to establish YWAM in India. My family soon moved south to the city of Chennai so I had no personal memories of Kolkata. What drew me back now for the first time since 1983 was a desire to understand this city so loved by my parents and other YWAMers — a city that asked unashamedly for love.*

*The media-manipulated image of Kolkata is one of devastating poverty. It is the city of Mother Teresa, a city of pressing crowds with outstretched hands asking for help. While aspects of this image are true, I knew there was something deeper than what the media portrayed. Friends told me of the Kolkata shining with India's literary and artistic heritage, a city bursting with color and culture.*

*Kolkata's sights and sounds greeted me the moment I stepped off the Express. Train whistles echoed off the station's high ceilings.*

*Vendors paced the platform, their shouts of "chai garam chai,[2]" "bread omelet," and "misti dhoi[3]" echoing among the departure announcements and final goodbyes. People brushed roughly past me, pushing onto crowded train cars. All along the station walls, bodies were stretched out, making their homes on the platform.*

*My first sights of the city itself were through the back window of a taxi, probably quite similar to those that greeted the first YWAMers back in 1982. Aging, intricately designed buildings dating from its days as capital of the British Raj soared above streets thriving with life. In just one block I saw scantily clad children begging for coins, an old man sitting on the pavement mending a shoe with a thread and needle, and a large shop window filled with glittering gold jewellery. Here the "have-nots" and the wealthy share living space.*

*A city built to accommodate a population of four million, Kolkata has ripped out its seams with a population of around 13 million. This eclectic citizenry varies from high-tech entrepreneurs in business suits to teens in designer jeans to Hindu priests in flowing robes. This mix of the old and the new symbolizes Kolkata, where a modern city is emerging through the yellowed lace of the old.*

*The next morning as I walked the city streets, I carried with me the stories of YWAMers who had lived here. Each of them saw beyond the dirt and clamor and suffering. They saw people loved by God and that stirred their hearts. They saw images of God in the smiles of street children, the pleas of lepers and beggars, in the weary eyes of mothers and fathers struggling to survive. It was here in Kolkata that the burden to reach out to "the least of these" was birthed. Believing something could be done, these YWAMers stayed.*

*One of them was a 20-year-old Californian named Elisabeth Cochrane (then Baumann), who arrived in Kolkata in 1981. An intense homesickness followed her initial culture shock. But despite this experience, she returned to Kolkata and through the years it has become for her a city filled with fond memories.*

*Elisabeth joined YWAM in 1979 in Kona, Hawaii, where she did a Discipleship Training School (DTS), followed by a School of Evangelism (SOE), after which she went to help pioneer the YWAM*

*Honolulu base. There she heard from Kalafi and Leda Moala and others of the spiritual need in South Asia. With Kalafi's support, Elisabeth and co-worker Judy Sproats flew to India and Nepal in July of 1981 to explore the possibilities of beginning a YWAM work there. She came for those few weeks purely out of obedience to God's word to her – not because she planned to live and work in these countries. But when she returned to Honolulu, she couldn't get those two countries out of her mind. She returned in 1982 to pioneer the work in Kolkata. In October of that same year, Elisabeth moved on to Kathmandu, Nepal, to pioneer YWAM there. She returned to India to staff YWAM's first DTS in January 1983, and then returned to Kathmandu. She remained there until December 1986 when she helped start new ministries with YWAM Mumbai (formerly Bombay). Today, she is married to Steve Cochrane and they are the parents of two daughters. The Cochranes serve as YWAM South and Central Asia's Field Directors, and Elisabeth also heads up the work of the University of the Nations in Pune, India (now located in Lonavala, an hour west of Pune). Here is Elisabeth Baumann's story of that first trip to Kolkata.*

# Out Among the Masses

I clung tightly to my suitcase as a smoke-belching truck blazed past us. Horns blasted continuously. The scorching sun threatened to melt us into the pavement. I had never felt so lost and out of place as this, my first day in Kolkata, India. To save money and because we didn't know how to find a hotel, my Australian co-worker Judy Sproats and I had set out walking from Kolkata's Dum Dum International Airport. We thought we could play it safe by walking in the general direction of the city. But with each step we grew more discouraged.

"I don't know if I can go any further," I told Judy. "My arms and back are aching, and it's so hot!"

"We've already been walking for an hour, and I doubt we're near wherever we're going." Judy agreed, wiping the sweat off her face with her shirtsleeve. We sat down precariously on our suitcases. People walked past, fixing their gaze on us.

"Elisabeth? Do you think we can take one of those buses into the city? I think they're local."

"I don't know." I pulled out my wallet and studied the purple, pink, and orange bills, trying to calculate the cost. "Maybe we do have enough to pay for a bus. We just need to make sure we have enough left over for the room and other expenses. I don't think I can walk anymore with this bag."

We picked up our bags and walked across the street to the bus stop. The streets were full of vehicles and not a single one stopped as I crossed the road, making for several close calls. I looked back as Judy was slowly making her way across, fear written all over her face.

Buses were pulling into the stop. Figuring they had to be heading into the city, we jumped on one and stood with our bags tucked between our legs. Inside people were packed into every possible space. Each time the bus stopped, hordes of people aggressively made their way on and off the bus. Once I was pushed against the seats, and the air was forced out of my lungs. Another thing that took my breath away was the smell of curries wafting in the bus from their roadside stalls. Thankfully this helped overpower the heavy smell of body odor. This was nothing like traveling on buses back in California.

As the bus moved slowly through the traffic, I peered over the heads of other riders, trying to get a glimpse at what we passed by. Men on bicycles furiously pedaled through the traffic. A cow lay on the divider between the lanes. People sat on the sides of the road, with fruit spread out before them on plastic sheets. One man wearing just a loincloth stood next to a roadside tap, his entire body covered in white suds. Nearby, children played, splashing each other with water, and then scattering in all directions.

The lady at my shoulder told me we could find somewhere to stay at the next stop, Sudder Street. So I grabbed Judy by the elbow, told her we had to get off, and rushed toward the door, luggage and all.

Sudder Street was lined with hotels, which looked more like apartment buildings with shops below. It took two or three tries before we found one we could afford. Our room had just two single beds and a bathroom.

"Well, at least we can sit down finally," I said, trying to be optimistic.

After washing up with a lukewarm bucket bath, I paused by the window to watch the sights below. Instantly a wave of homesickness passed through me. I brushed away a tear as I thought of my family back home. They were probably gathered around the dinner table, enjoying each other's company. I wanted to be with them. But I knew I had to pull myself together. Like so many newcomers to Kolkata I was coming face to face with the huge needs and everyday struggles of life in this great city.

"C'mon Judy, we need to call Kalafi and let him know we arrived safely."

We put some money in our pockets, locked the room and went to call Kalafi Moala. He had been the force behind getting Judy and I here. His vision was to see YWAM established in this part of the world, and I knew Judy and I were not the only ones he had exhorted about having a long-term vision for South Asia. I anticipated there were more to follow after us. I didn't think I would meet them, however, as I was returning to my life in the States. I imagined hearing from afar of YWAM's presence in India and Nepal in the near future.

Since YWAM had no presence in South Asia, Kalafi had no contacts he could put us in touch with. When we first approached him with the idea of coming here, he reacted with a mixture of excitement and nervousness. His zeal for meeting the spiritual needs of South Asia was tempered by fatherly concern about sending two young women alone into a new country. The only way he allowed us to go alone was with the promise that we would call him every few days to let him know we were okay. Other than that, we were on our own and had to learn the ropes of getting around in these two countries.

Out on the street we found a phone booth and dialled the

number. On the other end I heard a tone, and then silence. I tried the number again and again. Eight hours later — after several more sessions in that phone booth — we finally got through. As we walked back to our hotel, we were set upon by beggar children. One child insistently tugged on my shirt sleeve. My heart reached out to the hurtful look in her eyes. Were they a possible people group YWAM could reach out to if they were to come to India? There was a plea for mercy in her eyes. Finding a coin at the bottom of my purse, I pressed that in her hand, uttering a silent prayer that one day someone would minister to this little girl, both physically and emotionally, and many others like her. There were so many of them, and so few of us. The children, who had been watching on the sidelines, ran to my side, loudly insisting I give them money too. We didn't have money for all of them so Judy and I broke away and ducked into the hotel.

"Despite the craziness, I know God's hand is on all of this," Judy said, shaking her head in amazement.

"Yeah, Kalafi was kind of scared to send us here, but the Lord has taken care of us so far. Somehow we managed to get on the right bus and find an affordable place to stay. So here we are, halfway around the world. Hard to believe, isn't it?"

I pulled my journal out of my bag and began excitedly recording my experiences. I had left for this trip extremely optimistic about what lay ahead. Now everything I had seen here affected me emotionally. In just one day, incredible needs were thrust right before my eyes, both physical and spiritual. Nothing in my past experience could compare to this. I felt stripped of every tool I ever had for communication and coping. The day had been unforgettable, and I knew I wanted to record as much as possible of what had happened.

During our first days in Kolkata, we asked the Lord to guide our explorations of the city and to give us His heart for the nation. One place He guided me to was New Market, where many vendors sat on the sidewalks selling all types of goods. I still remember vividly one time when I was walking through the crowds there and knelt down to buy an orange. The vendor asked the purpose of my visit in Kolkata. I was surprised he spoke in English. Except for

Judy, I hadn't heard much English and was happy to tell him why we were here. As I talked to him, I felt I should share Jesus' love with him. We quickly attracted a crowd. That wasn't hard, us being two young white women. Perhaps the vendor sitting next to us had alerted others to what I was saying. Knowing I couldn't pass up this opportunity, I stood up from my crouching position next to the vendor, and shared what I had to say with the entire crowd. When I finished, people asked us for prayer, some stayed to have conversations with us about Jesus. Judy and I gladly obliged them.

With the crowd dispersed, we left to return to our room. My mind was full of what had happened outside New Market. The hunger I had seen in those eyes amazed me. Every one of them waited anxiously for my next word, like I was giving them a rare jewel. The image of faces from the crowd came before me and in my mind, I heard this Scripture echoed, "The harvest is plentiful, but the workers are few. Ask the Lord of the harvest, therefore, to send out workers into His harvest field" (Matthew 9:37-38). I began praying earnestly upon this verse. There was such a tremendous spiritual hunger among these precious people, and I prayed for workers to come soon to this region. Arriving here as two women in our early 20's had been such a big risk in itself, but I see now how it had served to pave the way. Others risk-takers would follow, planting more seeds and one day seeing those fruits ripen. I had no idea I would be one of the answers to my prayer.

When we returned to our room, I took my journal out of my bag to read what I had written the previous night. The last sentence I had written was, *"It would be so difficult if God ever called me here. Everything is so different to what I'm used to."* Little did I know I would return within the next year, and 25 years later I would still be here. When we returned to Honolulu after those fast-paced three weeks, Judy and I could not get all that we had seen out of our minds. I approached Kalafi, and shared how I felt I was to return to South Asia and work there for two years. Judy felt the same thing. We both returned to Kolkata a year later on the SOE team Steve Cochrane was leading. I stayed several months in India, networking with churches in Kolkata and staffing the DTS in Uluberia[4]. Judy stayed with me for nine months, then went on to help with the new YWAM work in Japan. I moved on to Kathmandu,

Nepal, where I worked until 1986. From there, Steve and I married in 1989 and moved to Mumbai and then to Pune to pioneer more new ministries.

As I look back, I can honestly say I am glad God called me to both India and Nepal. Although I now live in Pune, I treasure the memories of Kolkata. It was there that many of us developed a stronger burden and commitment for YWAM in this region of the world. Often, a newcomer to Kolkata is first struck by the poverty and crowds. As young foreigners we were also affected by that, but not in a negative way. We were ready to do whatever was necessary to help the poor. As a risk-taker, I quickly learned so much about the culture. And through that, God imparted to our hearts His own tremendous love for the nation of India.

2

# Small Beginnings

For years, I had longed to revisit the small village of Uluberia, site of YWAM India's first Discipleship Training School (DTS) and my family's first home in India. The place had taken on almost legendary qualities in my mind through the years as I listened to stories about that first school. Now a fresh excitement bubbled up as the train pulled into Kolkata's Howrah Station, and we squeezed into the women's compartment.

I was privileged to make this journey with two dear friends — Gill Simpson, who had been involved with the Uluberia base for several years, and Zipporah Tewes, who I had known for most of my years in India. Uluberia is just an hour's ride south of Kolkata, and 15 minutes after our train pulled out of the station, the metropolitan landscape of Kolkata gave way to rice and wheat fields and to thick groves of banana and palm trees. Only small clusters of huts broke up these long expanses of fields and forest. In the fields were women with baskets on their backs bending over to harvest the crops. Others fields had bare-chested men ploughing *behind a cart and bullock. The air out here felt "breathable," a welcome change from the smog and congestion of Kolkata!*

*At the Uluberia train station, we hailed cycle rickshaws and began the bumpy ride down what seemed to be the village's only paved road. We passed TV shops with cricket matches blaring on their sets, and other small shops selling biscuits, sweets, and rice. Ashoka and tamarind trees bordered both sides of the road, and beyond them were endless rice paddies. After less than ten minutes, the rickshaw stopped and the driver motioned for us to get out.*

*"Gill, is this it? I mean, where is the place?"*

*All I could see ahead of us was a lonely stretch of red brick road, winding toward more coconut trees and rice paddies.*

*"Yeah, this is it," she replied as she paid the driver. "We just have to walk down that lane a ways."*

*We followed the lane to a small compound surrounded by shoulder-high walls. Once off-white, the walls now were streaked with age splotches of yellow and black. The gate opened to a walkway leading to two blue-shuttered old buildings. Somehow this site of the first-ever India YWAM base was just as I imagined it.*

*"See the large building there on the right?" said Gill. "That is where the DTS students slept. The smaller one there on my left, that is where your parents probably lived." I looked closer at that building, racking my memory to see if I could remember what might have been my window. I couldn't. I was only three years old when we lived here.*

*Behind these two buildings was a smaller one. There was no door, just a dark hollow space. Gill said that was the kitchen. Its walls appeared permanently blackened from years of cooking over open coals.*

*Walking through the rickety screen doors of the main building, Gill called into the dark hallway, "Hello? Is anyone here? Mr. Biswas?"*

*An old couple shuffled toward us. She leaned on him, as he leaned on a cane. Gill stepped forward to greet them, and was met with smiles and affectionate pats on her cheek.*

*Nodding to me, she said, "This is Sonya. Remember Tim and Karol Svoboda? This is their daughter, the oldest one. And this is Zippu, her friend."*

*With no signs of recollection, they sat down slowly on cane chairs behind the room's one desk. We took our seats opposite them on rusted metal folding chairs. Mrs. Biswas locked her gaze on me for a time. Then, her face brightened.*

*"Ah, yes," she said. "I remember now. Remember Tiger? The dog?"*

*I didn't quite remember Tiger, but I had heard of him, so I nodded my head.*

*"You and your sister were the only ones Tiger actually liked. I remember Tiger bit one of the students when he stepped over him. Tiger didn't like that and snapped at him!" Mrs Biswas's shoulders shook as she laughed to herself about the incident.*

*The Biswas were now the only inhabitants of the compound. As we visited, I probed for more memories of what it was like back in 1983. I wondered how the experience of hosting that first DTS might have affected them.*

*The chatter of those young missionaries would have filled every room. The shouts and exuberances of praise would have seemed 'other-worldly' in their quiet environment. The students would have scurried back and forth between the buildings, carrying large pots of hot dahl and rice to the dining room. They would have carried buckets of water and mops to begin their work duties. Probably the only quiet time of the day was when people were sleeping. I wondered if the Biswas' were happy in this ghostly silent compound or if they ever had a longing for the noise and busyness of those days to return. From the look of it, the compound had changed little since 1983, but being on site could only take me so far in understanding what had happened within these walls. For the deeper story I knew I would need to talk to the one person who remembered it most vividly — Steve Cochrane.*

*Steve was first introduced to YWAM as a teen-ager when he*

*participated in an outreach to the Montreal Olympic Games in 1976. It was there that the youth from Tacoma, Washington, felt the Lord was calling him to missions. He joined YWAM Tacoma in 1979, and first met Kalafi Moala when he came to Tacoma to speak in their DTS. Kalafi quickly saw the leadership potential in Steve, and started recruiting him to work with YWAM in Honolulu. In 1981, Steve joined Kalafi's team which included future South Asia pioneers Brad Carr, Elisabeth Baumann (Steve's future wife), Judy Sproats, and Tim and Karol Svoboda.*

*At a Honolulu staff conference, YWAM founder Loren Cunningham exhorted the staff to "Go West" (meaning Asia). At that time it seemed to Steve that the doors to Asia were closed for him. But two days later, while Kalafi was speaking to the staff, Steve began thinking of Kolkata and couldn't get India out of his mind. He said to God that day, "Lord, I am willing to go to Kolkata." When he told Kalafi what happened, Kalafi's response was, "Brother, this is it!" An SOE team was about to leave in two weeks for an outreach to Kolkata and without hesitation Kalafi appointed Steve to lead the team. In August 1982, Steve and his team landed in Kolkata, where he began the first steps of pioneering YWAM. He knew the key to establishing YWAM was training Indian workers and he believed the way to do this was to run a DTS. In January 1983, that first DTS was started in Uluberia. Twenty plus years later, Steve remains in India. He now lives in Pune with his wife, Elisabeth, and their two daughters. Currently, he is the Field Director for South and Central Asia. Here in his own words is an account of those simple, beginning days in Uluberia.*

# Challenges of the First DTS

Brad Carr and I arrived in Kolkata, eager to get started. Waiting for us was Wendy Mahbert, an adventurous young Nepali woman, who had heard about YWAM through a traveling recruiter and had gone by faith all the way to Singapore to attend DTS. One of her speakers in that school was Kalafi Moala. He encouraged Wendy to help start a DTS in India, and she rose to the challenge. Wendy proved to be an invaluable member of our team, as she helped us through many of our cultural blunders and set us back on path. As a team, our goal was to run a DTS by January 1983. We wanted to see Indians take the gospel throughout India. They were to be the torch bearers.

Now that it was actually happening, we realized the planning stage was the easier part. Starting the DTS was one upset after another. A building was secured in Kolkata, and the first payment was made. Then without warning, the landlord decided not to rent to us and took the building out of our hands. Hearing of our desperation, a friend in Kolkata recommended we try a former Baptist missionary compound in Uluberia.

A group went out there, returning with stories of a beautiful property surrounded by ponds and trees just outside a small village. Unfortunately, there was another interested tenant, the Assemblies of God (AG) church in Kolkata. Because they had the necessary finances, it seemed likely that they would be the next tenants. As always, we were trusting God to bring in the money for our rent.

Brad and I went to the AG church, the same day the landlord Mr. Biswas was coming to meet with the AG pastor. While the two men negotiated on a price, Brad and I sat in the opposite room praying. While we prayed, I felt a strong impression that the compound in Uluberia was to be ours. I looked up to see Brad had stopped praying. He told me he had the same impression about Uluberia. As if on cue, the door opened and the AG pastor entered the room. "You guys are going to be able to use Uluberia," he said cheerfully, as if he were a partner and not a contender for the Uluberia site. We rented it that very day.

The DTS was set to begin in three days so we didn't have a moment to lose in our preparations. The next morning we boarded the suburban train and rode out to Uluberia, armed with mops, brooms and buckets. Our motley group of youthful foreigners along with one Indian and one Nepali must have made quite an unusual sight to the Indian passengers.

We finished the cleaning late in the evening of the same day.

Wendy and Elisabeth refreshed us that evening with steaming pots of rice and vegetable curry. Setting them on the floor, our weary crew gathered around to give thanks and to eat by candlelight on the cold stone floor. As we ate our meager meal, I wondered how our ridiculously low budget would provide for all of the 18 students that were expected to come in tomorrow. Only God knew, and we had seen His faithfulness too many times to doubt.

On arrival day, we enthusiastically waited for our new students to appear. Raghavendra Gupta was one of the first. Ragha, as we called him, was born into a high-caste family of Brahmin Hindus, but was raised by Catholic nuns. Ragha had been a sickly infant and his mother had visited Hindu temples around the country in an attempt to cure him. As Ragha edged closer to death, she took him to St. Anne's Hospital, near Kolkata, in an act of desperation. A doctor there pronounced his case hopeless so the mother placed her son on a baby scale and walked out. A concerned nurse named Sister Isabel took Ragha home, baptized him according to Catholic beliefs, and nursed him back to health. Within three months, Ragha had gained weight and his health was restored. Sister Isabel raised him; having convinced his parents God had a sovereign plan for his life.

At 17, Ragha came to Kolkata in search of job and found work as a tea server at a roadside restaurant. Since it was close to our guesthouse, we ate at this restaurant almost every day. Our group of foreigners aroused Ragha's curiosity, and one day he asked if he could talk to us. He wanted to know the reason behind the obvious joy on our faces. We told him about Jesus, and he was eager to know more about Christianity. Ragha had a break each day from three to five in the afternoon, so he and I started to meet each day during this time. Three weeks into these meetings, I asked him if he would like to become a Christian. He said yes. Once we prayed together, I ran all the way back to the guest house to tell the others of Ragha's declaration. Seeing him here in Uluberia thrilled me, and I was looking forward to being a part of his journey as a Christian.[5]

His arrival, as well as the arrival of two others, was the only encouraging sign on that first day. Were all the application forms nothing? Had people just signed but had no commitment in mind?

Discouragement weighing heavily upon me, I walked to the small red church at the front of the compound where they were having their meeting to welcome the students.

Most of the students and staff were seated, but even in this small church our numbers looked paltry. *Is this our DTS? What will happen to our great vision of YWAM in this country? It can't possibly start on such a small foundation. India is such a large country, we need a larger foundation.* All day I had been wrestling with these types of thoughts. As I walked to the front, it took all I had within me to trust that something good would come out of this.

"Well, here we are." I said, looking over the faces gathered in the front pew. Ragha looked at me expectantly, eager to soak up more about Christianity. Ragha was the only new Christian among the three students. Ian, an Indian of Chinese descent, had grown up in a Christian family. I found him to be an intense young man, whose eyes radiated his excitement about the DTS. Daniel Lingwood, an Anglo Indian, had also grown up in the church. All three of these students were from the city of Kolkata.

"Let's just start out the meeting in prayer. We will seek the Lord on what He would like to say to us. I don't really have an agenda for this meeting." The room was quiet, except for an occasional shuffle, as heads were bowed and people prayed.

*Don't despise the day of small beginnings*[6] repeatedly came to my mind. *What on earth does that mean, God?* Again it came, *Don't despise the day of small beginnings.* I lifted my head to look at the small group gathered. All day long the thought of canceling the DTS kept running through my head. It was back again now as I looked over the three students sitting together on the front pew and then at the staff. They were truly a tiny group, but they were incredible men and women of God.

*God, do you mean you are going to do something out of this small beginning?* I asked. When I walked into this church, I was so discouraged that I was ready to cancel this DTS we all had worked so hard to bring about. Now, with these whispered words, I knew without a doubt we were to continue this DTS, whether it had three people in it or the promised 18 people. It was going to continue because something exciting was ahead. A week later, we had 16 students, confirming that God had indeed spoken.

Two months after that encouraging word, the Lord had another surprise for us: a visitation by an angel. It came at a very low point in my life, when I was sick and weak and discouraged. Sickness was becoming quite common for me and other staff, but we pushed through, not letting the sickness stop us from participating in the wonderful things God was doing in the school.

One night in March, I lay in bed with dysentery. My stomach twisted inside me, while a fever sapped any remaining strength. I pulled the thin sheet tighter around me to ward off the chills. Only a few minutes ago, I had been sweating. This fever just wouldn't leave me. By now, I had lost count of my trips to the toilet.

Through my fever-fogged mind, I heard the Lord ask me to worship Him. Not just me, but all of us as a group. I dragged myself out of bed, and wrapped the thin sheet tightly around my body. It was March, a mildly warm night. Nevertheless, I shivered as I walked through the overgrown grass and on the uneven cobblestones to the main building where I knew most people would be. I told those there what the Lord wanted us to do. As they dispersed to spread the news, I took a place against the wall and waited for people to come.

In several minutes, we sat in a circle on the floor. Solomon Rai, a student gifted in worship, led us into the Lord's presence. I looked around the circle, people's eyes were closed and hands uplifted as some were in prayer and others singing songs. I leaned against the white-washed wall to try to ease the aches throughout my body and pulled the thin sheet tighter against my body. I mouthed the words to the songs, trying to will my heart to follow suit. My strength was drained away, and my head began to droop toward my chest. I caught myself and sat up straight, jerking my head upright, looking toward the doorway. There in the hollow of the door, a person stood. His head was held high, only inches beneath the top frame of the door. Dressed all in white, he carried a large sword at his side.

All of a sudden, I felt my body propelled forward, until I was laying face down on the floor. I don't know how long I was down on the floor. But when I got up, the aches, fever, and stomach pains were gone. I was renewed and whole. My eyes searched for the mysterious visitor, but he no longer stood in the doorway. Still stunned by what I had seen and experienced, I left that night without telling anyone a word about it. I wondered if what I had seen was a hallucination.

But I was reminded of an incident that made me certain that what I had seen was an angel. Just a year earlier, I had met YWAM leader Paul Hawkins at an Asian staff conference in Korea. I approached Paul then, asking him to prayerfully commission me into the work of establishing YWAM India. During this time of prayer, he received a word for our team. The word was that the angel of the Lord would go before us with a sword.

At breakfast, I had another surprise waiting for me. Pam Blackburn, an elderly Canadian lady, was excitedly addressing all those sitting around the table. "It's amazing what happened to me at three 'o clock this morning. I saw an angel!" Shocks of electricity raced up and down my spine. Leaning forward, I asked her, "Can you describe what he looked like?"

"Well, he was dressed all in white and carried a sword. He was very tall and he was standing right over there." I followed her finger, and it was pointing right at the door where I had seen the angel last night.

The Angel never said anything. The Angel never gave any reassuring word that our breakfast would be provided for the next morning or that some of these DTS students would one day become the pillars of our ministry or that he would provide more staff. But it was the mere presence of the Angel that brought tears to our eyes. These tears were birthed out of the overwhelming knowledge that God was walking alongside us, that He had already gone before us, and that He would be both our healer and our protector.

The Angel never appeared again, but he left with us the reassurance that no matter how hard things seemed, God was with us every step of the way. Our weaknesses would become strengths through Him and Him alone.

**3**

# A Humble Walk
# Toward New Life

*A* *ah, yes, that first DTS. It really was a milestone." How often I had heard that comment from YWAMers who were part of the first school in Uluberia. While all agree that it was significant, it affected them all in very different ways. Staff and students alike had no idea what lay ahead as the DTS began, and all had to work through individual challenges that shook them physically, spiritually and emotionally. When they were at one of their lowest points, the appearance of the angel gave all a renewed sense of assurance that God had not forgotten them. They all walked through their various struggles, holding tightly to the Father's hand, as children hold onto their earthly father's hand. They held on in the belief that lives would be transformed. And eventually they were.*

*One of Steve Cochrane's visions for YWAM India was to see Indians become an integral part of the mission. He put this vision into action soon after arriving in Kolkata. He poured his life into the Indian students who came for that first DTS, and several of them remain in YWAM 23 years later). Some hold prominent leadership positions. Collectively these DTS students became major foundation stones of YWAM India and people of great influence in their nation.*

*While I was on the Uluberia compound in November 2003, I tried to imagine what it was like for the Indians involved in that first DTS. There must have been a lot of anxiousness about cultural differences, about what these foreigners expected of them, and what the future held for them together. The staff was anxious too because of the pioneering nature of the school, but there was also tremendous excitement from knowing they were on the threshold of a new frontier. Most students came out of an eager desire to know God, but were also watching carefully to see if the actions of these foreigners matched their words. This cultural context of a staff that was mainly foreign and students who were all Indian did produce some conflicts but ultimately Jesus broke through those dividing walls to forge lifetime friendships.*

*Later in 2003, I traveled around India to interview some of these former students. One was Narendra Tiwari. His story is one I won't ever forget. As we talked, I was struck by the realization that this man who had playfully carried me around on his shoulders when I was a child was someone clearly set apart by God as a vessel of change in his nation.*

*Narendra was born in Uttar Pradesh as a Brahmin – India's highest caste — and was trained to follow in his father's footsteps as a Hindu priest. Narendra's father taught him to be distrustful of foreigners. He even discouraged his son's English training at school because he saw it as throwback to colonialism. Despite his rank and privileges, Narendra grew increasingly dissatisfied with his life. He was bitter about being forced into an arranged marriage at age 13, and grew cold and cruel in his actions toward others. But all changed after he met some Christians living in his area and attended one of their meetings. From a human perspective, Narendra's entrance into YWAM was more accidental than intentional. But in God's kingdom, there are no accidents. Here is Narendra Tiwari's story in his own words.*

# First Fruits of the DTS

A small-framed man knelt before me, his head nearly touching the floor. He was pleading with me to divine for him where to find his lost buffalo.

"Go. Wash yourself. Don't come back until you're clean."

When he returned, I opened my book. I found an appropriate design and asked him to place his hand on the design, and close his eyes. While he did so, I calculated some figures in my head, deducing as to which direction the buffalo might have gone.

"The buffalo has gone that way," I pointed in the eastern direction of the village, "but someone else has found it. He will refuse to return the buffalo to you."

The man's shoulders dropped.

"You must buy a new buffalo."

"Thank you," he raised his pressed palms to his chest, took a few steps backwards and walked away.

I snapped my fingers, and a small boy came running to give me a handkerchief so I could wipe the sweat off my face. This was a typical day for me. My father was training me to become a priest like him. Together we worshipped Durga, the goddess of death. Every afternoon, people came to my house to hear their futures. By mathematical equations and analyzing diagrams, I foretold their destinies.

I was treated as a god, but at home there was no love. My father beat me over minor issues. This life was all I had known, but inside I longed for acceptance and love. I tried to find my own answers in the designs and mathematical equations, but never could. It was frustrating not to know my own future. At age 17, the desire to know what lay ahead grew increasingly urgent. I wondered if I would be famous. Would I have many disciples underneath me? Was I to be blessed with many sons? What would I come back to earth as in my next life?

In desperation, I turned elsewhere to find answers. Many of

my friends were gangsters, and I robbed along with them to be accepted. I also tried to find answers in joining a radical Hindu group and the Communist party. But nothing filled the emptiness in my heart.

One Sunday my friends invited me to go with them to talk to Santosh Das, a Christian farmer. They wanted to tease him about the strange things he had been saying. Having nothing better to do, I went with them. We found him in his fields, pushing the plough, and immediately started to ridicule him. But he answered each of the comments calmly, never becoming mad at us. In my heart I knew what we were doing was wrong and told my friends to leave. I wanted to talk to Santosh alone. When my friends left, I found it hard to talk to him calmly because of the pride in my heart. Santosh said to me, "Mr. Tiwari, I'm not saying you must leave your family, religion, parents, society, culture and luxurious life. You can do everything, but I just want to tell you that God is going to judge you one day. Are you ready to give an answer in front of Him?"

"Who do you think you are talking to? Our 34 million gods can judge or kill anyone. My religion says that man's spirit is god, so I am god. I know how to judge people. I will go to heaven by doing good things."

As I lay in bed that night, I kept thinking about what this man had said to me. How could he say one day I would be judged? If I am god, how is it I do both good and bad? Who is this god that is going to judge me?

The next morning, I returned to Santosh.

"Don't give me a lecture. Just tell me the name of the god who will judge me."

"Narendra," Santosh said, laying his plough carefully on the ground, "This God's name is Jesus Christ. He is the only God, there are no other gods."

I kept quiet, but inside I was wondering how he could say something like this. How could he say there was only one god! What was wrong with him?

"It is through Jesus Christ that we can go to heaven, not because of good deeds," he continued. Then he closed his eyes, and started talking to this God of his. He asked for him to reveal Himself to me. I looked at his face, he was crying! *What had I done?* Now I was afraid.

He lifted his head, wiped the tears from his eyes, and said, "We have a cottage meeting in our home, would you like to come?" I said yes, out of curiosity. But already I knew I was doing something that could get me into big trouble. This man was a low-caste, he was very poor, and I was a Brahmin. We weren't supposed to associate with low-caste people.

But I went anyways. What I found there was love and acceptance like I had never experienced before. In my neighborhood, people seemed to be constantly arguing and fighting. But here people gathered together in one room in such peace and unity. I wanted to learn this group's secret.

I returned home, and my father was waiting for me. Somehow he had found out where I had been. Rising out of his chair, he walked toward me, "What's wrong with my religion that you went there to learn from those Christians? I can teach you many things here. What else do you need?"

I answered him with what I had learned this evening. My father and I had never talked about Christianity before, and his anger flared as we talked. In his hand was a garden spade, and he told me to hold out my left hand. When I did, he beat it until my left hand became paralyzed.

"Go outside, now!" he said. He pulled my clothes off, except my lunghi, and pushed me outside. It was December and very cold.

"Bend over," he shouted. "You have two choices. I will put these bricks on your back. If one falls off, I will add another. Your second choice is to renounce this Jesus of yours. Never go to those meetings anymore. If you agree to stop going, I will stop beating you." With that, he beat me with the bricks on my back. My father is very strong and with each beating, I fell down and the bricks fell with them. He shouted at me to renounce Jesus. I didn't want to. So he put more bricks on my back and hit me again with the spade. I was convinced the love I had experienced this evening could not be found anywhere else. The skin on my back was breaking open, but he continued to beat me.

In my mind, I cried out, "Oh God, why is this happening?"

I heard a quiet voice saying *leave now, run!* It had to be Jesus. There was no strength left in me, but I tried. I stumbled to the ground. My father stood over me and continued to beat me. Again, I heard the small voice telling me to run. I picked myself up, and this time I got away. Fear kept me running, but the pain shooting through my body blinded me from any clear direction. I found myself inside a muddy ditch, shivering from cold and fear.

Only a few hours ago, I had everything. I had servants, I had respect, and I had a luxurious life. Now all I had was a lunghi. I thought about ending my life, but then I remembered the farmer, Santosh, and decided to make my way to his place and see if he could help me.

It was already one-thirty in the morning when I crawled out of the ditch. By now, the blood had dried along with the mud. It was painful to walk, but I pressed on shivering in the cold night air. Those Christians said their God cared about me. Now I would see if they were telling the truth.

I continued walking, weaving behind the houses to stay out of the sight of prying eyes. The moon was still a small sliver. But it seemed the night had become brighter. Was it the stars? No, something was different. Up ahead of me, I saw a large star shining. It was moving! Moving closer to me. As I walked, it followed me, coming in closer. I thought I was going to die. I thought it was going to fall on top of me, crush me. Did my father curse me? Did he call this star to kill me? I tried to move out of its path of light, but it continued straight ahead of me, as if to shine a path for me. Somehow, I sensed I was meant to follow this star, but I was scared. After what seemed like the longest and most fearful walk of my life, the star stopped. It was shining its light on the same house where I had met those Christians.

I walked up to the door and knocked. Santosh opened it to find me covered in blood and mud. As soon he recognized who I was, he started to cry. He pulled me inside and immediately bathed me and bandaged my wounds. After this, we left on the back of his bicycle to a safer place. Within a month, Jesus had healed the wounds on my body. For six months, He kept me safely hidden from my father.

But when my father found me, he forced me to return with him and kept me locked up in a room with no window, light, or fan. This was during the summer time, so it was very hot. Six guards made sure I could not escape. Astrologers came to visit me, food offered to the gods was given to me, all in a vain attempt to cure me of my new beliefs. On the ninth day I managed to climb out onto the roof and escape. I ran, unsure where I was going. I came to a river where the Hindus cremated their dead. It was a very unclean place for a Brahmin, but I felt I had no option but to cross it. I prayed to God to give me the strength, as I swam across the river, and then walked to a Christian friend's house.

I was soon given the chance to attend the Assemblies of God Bible College in Bihar, the state neighboring Uttar Pradesh. At the end of the second year, one of my old disciples saw me there and told my father. Although he didn't succeed in making me return home with him, he published my photo in the newspaper. Under the photo was an order for anyone who saw me to shoot me.

While I was in Bihar, I attended a Pentecostal church where I was baptized. At each step of my journey, I saw my Heavenly Father's provision and protection over me. There was a peace I found in Him, and His power was greater than anything I had studied or experienced. I was relishing the experience of God's love and the love of other Christians, but in my heart, I still harbored pride. I did not completely understand what it meant to follow Jesus. There was still so much for me to learn.

Even though I had just one more year to complete for my degree, I knew I had to leave Bihar soon. My identity was now public knowledge; it was too risky to stay. In December 1982, I moved to Kolkata and found refuge with a pastor there. He told me about YWAM's school for young Christians in Uluberia and said this school would teach me more about how to be a Christian. So I enrolled in the DTS in January 1983 — two years after I left home.

When I arrived, I wondered what I had gotten myself into with this group of people and their strange behavior. I felt like I had been thrown into a world where every belief I grew up with was challenged. My English was not so good, and this added to my struggles.

These foreigners – mostly Americans — washed dishes and cleaned floors just like ordinary household servants. The day I arrived, Elisabeth Baumann, was the first person to greet me. She showed me to my room, which was bare except for a few rolled up mattresses. Elisabeth apologized for the dirt on the floor and began to sweep it away. I leaned against the doorpost, speechless and shocked. Once I could collect myself, I asked where the servants were. She said, "We have none." I could only wonder what kind of place I had come to.

I set my one bag down next to the only spare mattress. I had arrived late. A tall, skinny white man walked into the room. He looked young, but was already slightly bald. He walked up and said, "You must be Narendra, I am Steve," and shook my hand vigorously.

He placed his hand gently on my shoulder, "Narendra, I want to introduce you to these students. Guys, this is Narendra. He is from Kolkata." It was good Steve said that. What if Steve had said I was from Balia (my hometown)? The news surely would have reached my father.

"This is Ian." Ian stuck his hand out. "He's also from Kolkata."

He was a Chinese-Indian. As he looked at me, he seemed like a very serious person.

"And this is Ragha." Steve said, moving across the room. Ragha looked like a young boy. His black hair flopped on his head as he greeted me, palms pressed to his chest. I greeted him likewise.

"Where are you from in Kolkata?" Ian asked.

I mentioned where the pastor had lived, hoping he wouldn't ask more questions.

"The others aren't here. But you'll meet them soon. So glad you're here." With that, Steve walked out the room.

I sat down on my mattress, cross-legged. Ian's and Ragha's mattresses had sheets neatly spread on them. Maybe someone would come and spread sheets on my bed as well. I stared at them, trying to see what type of people they were. They seemed friendly, but why would they come to a place like this?

I left the room and walked back out through the dark hallway. Steve sat at the small desk, hunched over a pile of papers. Next to him, a plate of rice and dahl sat. He ate, while looking through his papers. My stomach groaned reminding me it had been a couple of hours since I had last eaten. As I entered he looked up with a large smile, saying, "Have you settled in okay, Narendra?"

"Yes. Thank you." I stood there for a couple of seconds, hoping Steve would offer me something to eat. I could not ask him.

"We have a meeting now. I will walk with you over to the church." Steve gulped down one last bite. We walked silently, but inside I was seething. Steve seemed to be such a gentle man. How could he be so rude as to eat in front of me and not offer me anything? How strange these foreigners were!

At the church, Steve made a few announcements and then started to talk about God's love, His provision, and how glad He was to have us all here. I could not listen. How could he talk about love, about living for God, when he couldn't share? Maybe all the negative things my father had said about foreigners were true. Did these foreigners think they could come to our country and disrespect us like this?

In closing, Steve announced that each of us would be assigned certain "work duties," such as mopping floors, cleaning bathrooms, washing dishes. I sat up straight and listened now. We were students. Why should we have to work? Steve said it would put into practice what we learned in the classroom, things like servant leadership, humility and teamwork.

I bolted back to my room when Steve dismissed the meeting. It was dark and empty. No one had made my bed so I lay down on the bare mattress and willed myself to sleep. After lectures the next day, I walked by the kitchen on my way to workduties. Clang! Bang! *That must be Ragha in there!* Ragha, a former chai vendor in Kolkata , was a fellow student here in Uluberia. He cooked meals for his 'work duty'. Each day he banged the dishes around, trying to send a loud message that he would rather be elsewhere. I laughed to myself, but only for a short while. I soon remembered my own work duty: scrubbing floors. If my father could see me now, he would have a good laugh. He would say, *'See Narendra, see what this Jesus did to you, He is making you clean floors.'*

When I first arrived, I was thankful for this remote place. I felt safe here in this old Baptist compound hidden amongst trees and ponds. But each day as I scrubbed the floors, I grew more resentful of the leaders' disrespect for my position as a Brahmin. I was also unhappy to learn that a woman would be teaching on holiness for a whole week. What did they know about holiness?

The woman — Wendy Mahbert from Nepal — moved around the class in short, accented movements. Her black hair bounced and her eyes shone like fire. With swift, strong swipes, her hands emphasized every point she made. Though less than five feet tall, her shrill voice thundered like a giant. I was not interested in listening to a woman. She was not born with the right to stand in front of the class and tell me what I must do to be holy.

I had studied holiness. Who was to say that this woman had any training on the topic? It was I who had the training. It was I who knew what a person must go through to obtain holiness.

When she finished talking she dismissed us saying, "Have a good lunch. We have our specialty, dahl and rice!" Some students laughed. We had dahl and rice almost everyday! Taking her files into her arms she walked out of the classroom. I hurried out the door, following her.

"Excuse me! Wendy! May I talk to you?" my breath came in short gasps, from running after her.

"Yes, Narendra?" her smile was pleasant, maybe too pleasant.

"How can you say I must be holy? Why are you saying things like that? Do you know who I am? I can listen to talk about love and faith but I cannot sit and listen to you talk about holiness in. . ."

"What do you mean?" she said, switching her files to her arm.

"You know who I am? I trained to be a Hindu priest. I know about holiness."

"We're talking about Christian holiness, not Hindu holiness."

"But what? No, you aren't understanding this!"

Wendy was rooted to the spot. I looked down at her; there were tears in her eyes. Now she was crying!

"Why are you crying? Stop crying." Her crying was making me mad.

"Narendra, we will talk later, okay?" she said quietly, her head down. I walked away, shaking my head. I could not listen to her talk like that. Who was she? She was only a woman. She should not be crying! Maybe now she would stop talking about holiness.

I knew I had earned the authority to speak on holiness. I couldn't understand how this woman could stand at the front and talk about holiness. I couldn't understand how she could be roaming amongst so many foreigners, she was a Nepali. She was also too young to be in leadership. I didn't like anything about her. Many times I tried to talk to her, to tell her that I didn't agree with her. I just walked away in frustration. But she never stopped talking about holiness to the class.

I scrubbed harder at the spot on the floor. It wouldn't come off. So I moved on, dragging my knees across the floor. That morning they announced that at the end of the three months we would leave on outreach. I had never heard of that word before. During outreach we were supposed to put into practice what we had learned in all these lectures. We learned much about servant leadership. This concept really confused me. How could I be a leader and help clean up the classrooms? I still didn't understand how love could make a person do what was required by the Christian faith: submission, humility, servanthood.

The 16 students would split into two teams and go share this Christian faith with others. Witnessing, telling others about the Christian faith, I just couldn't do. I first thought, sure if they just let me speak on holiness then I can do it, not all this other stuff, I don't understand it. But holiness I can teach others about.

The cloth in my hand was soggy. The skin on my fingers wrinkled. I had enough of this floor mopping. The floor wasn't finished. The staff knew I was fasting and would excuse me from work. I did not like work duties. I couldn't stand this work duty; someone like me should not have to do it. At home, the servants did everything; they brought food, they cooked, they cleaned. I was only expected to be a good son, and this included training to become a Hindu priest. One day Ragha and Ian dragged me out of bed, demanding why I didn't want to work. I tried saying I was too tired, but that didn't satisfy them. So I thought if I fasted, then I would be excused from work duties. This was something surely everyone would understand. Seeing my weak state, they would not make me work. So I said I would fast two meals every day for forty days. Steve was very kind and excused me from work duties. He wanted to know the purpose of my fast. I told him I would be praying for the staff and students to become more mature and holy. But I couldn't resist my hunger and sometimes slipped away to the shops to buy food when no one noticed. Today was one of the rare days I had to mop the floor.

When outreach time arrived, I was still skeptical about these YWAM people. Our team went to North India. For the majority of the time we stayed in a small fishing village in the state of Orissa. The men left before the sun rose. Their boats were long, narrow and flat on top. Once they reached the deep part of the sea, they stood up, and cast their nets over the water, waiting until the fish came. Later in the morning, the men would return. Then the women would clean the fish, and select the best for the market. Sometimes they did not keep any fish for themselves because giving everything to the market would bring in a larger profit for them. Their style of life was harsh. They depended on the sea for their livelihood, and it wasn't always kind to them. But still they graciously accepted us into their homes.

During the rare occasions that we had free time, I walked along the beach. The fishermen's huts were closely tucked to the shoreline. Nets were laid out across the sand to dry. The sand was warm and soft below my feet. I walked along the shore, careful not to get my feet wet, thinking about what I had seen during the day. It was so different from my life in Balia. Here people worked in order to survive. Back in Balia, these people would work so we could live. Now here I was, living just like they were, and I was not here to be served by them. So many times in the lectures they had told us that we had come to serve.

Inside my heart, another wall broke within this small fishing village in Orissa. It was here God convicted me of my attitude. I clung to what I had been taught as a Brahmin. During Bible School, I thought the message of forgiveness and holiness was not for me, but for others. I clung to this attitude during DTS, often exerting this pride on Wendy. The last three months had been such a struggle. I still found the English language difficult. I still had a hard time accepting these foreigners completely. I did not want to come on this outreach, but that wasn't an option. I felt like a quiet observer. I thought I had something to give these people. I thought I could teach them something about holiness because of my background. But these people had something to teach me. As I watched their lives, I saw how Jesus would have lived among people like these. He would have gone on their boats with them. He would have sat on the beach with them, helping them empty the nets and place the fish into baskets. When He walked on the earth, He did not ask for any special favors. But He lived like those around Him, taking an interest in every part of their lives. Jesus, the great God, came and lived with simple people like these. He could have lived with people of royal heritage. He could have lived like a Brahmin, like me, but instead He chose to live with fishermen. He chose this lifestyle because of His love.

After all this time of running, I was finally beginning to understand the mystery of this religion. God opened up the English language for me, and I began to understand more of the language as well as the YWAMers. I saw YWAM in a new way and what they did became attractive to me. During my time with the YWAMers, I experienced God's love in a very real way. Another wall of my resistance was demolished in the small fishing village of Orissa. I left the DTS and continued my degree at the Bible College in Bihar. While there, I received a letter from Tim Svoboda. I was shocked and touched that he remembered me, considering he only came during the last three weeks of our DTS lecture phase in Uluberia. In the letter he was inviting me to attend an SOE (School of Evangelism) in Chennai. After completing my degree, I went to Chennai. I have remained with YWAM since then. I am the insider, no longer the skeptical outsider.

At the early age of 13 I had been married to Kalandi. I was angry with this marriage. When I ran away from my father, I gave no thought to her. But after the DTS, God prodded me to reunite with her. My YWAM brothers and sisters prayed and fasted while I traveled back to my village to reconcile and bring her to Kolkata. My father was happy to see me, but incensed when he discovered my real reason. I am convinced it was through the prayers of my brothers and sisters that my father never laid a hand upon me or threatened me in any way. I was able to bring Kalandi to Kolkata without any trouble. Three years later in November 1989, she was baptized in Christ's Holy Spirit and continues to serve faithfully by my side.

Today, I have returned to Varanasi. As the holy city of India, this city is replete with reminders from my past. These reminders have not deterred me from the Christian faith; rather my faith is stronger as I see the needs of my community. During my years here I have seen some incredible spiritual breakthroughs. Today I am working with a tribal group called the Bhoj Puri. In this group I have been privileged to share the Gospel and also to plant 25 churches. Now I am in the process of constructing a building which will serve as a refuge for widows. Within the Hindu society, when a woman's husband dies, she is no longer considered useful in society. Often, she is sent back to her family and treated as if her husband's death was her own fault. It is hard for Hindu widows to regain a sense of dignity as they are treated as low-caste. My aim in having this shelter for them is to provide this place of refuge so as to restore their dignity. Sometimes I have to marvel at God's plan, taking me as a former Brahmin to the place of ministry I serve in today. He has truly brought me a long way from who I formerly was.

4

# A Foothold in Nepal

*y family had been in India six months when YWAM called its first-ever conference for South Asia. At the time, this included just India and Nepal, and the total number of workers was 20 —most of them barely out of their teens. The meeting was held near Kathmandu, Nepal, where a determined young couple, James and Jean Smith, were struggling to establish the mission in an isolated country noted for its towering mountains.*

*In the 22 years since YWAM Nepal began, the country is much changed. Its great mountains now attract thousands of foreign tourists and trekkers. The royal family retains power, but a democratic party now governs Nepal. [In February 2005, the king dissolved the government and declared a state of emergency which is still in effect] And the spiritual oppression that once ruled the country has eroded significantly, thanks to the work of YWAM, other mission organizations, and courageous Nepali Christians.*

*It is still illegal to convert people to Christianity. Nepal has long forbidden its citizen's involvement in any form of mission activities. Despite this, Nepalis joined YWAM, risking disownment from their family and punishment from the government. The penalty for a person who converted from Hinduism to another religion was one year in jail. For a person caught preaching the Gospel, it was a six year imprisonment. In 1990, a democratic revolution swept through Nepal, and over 65 religious cases were dismissed. Throughout the nation, a spirit of freedom was rising. Fear left people's hearts. The doors for YWAM Nepal opened wider.*

*But James and Jean's first seven years in the country was a daily effort to keep their work discreet. Their remaining in the country for 17 years is a testimony to God's protection and blessing upon their work.*

*Because of the great distance between Nepal and our home in Chennai, I did not have the opportunity to spend time with the Smiths during my growing up years in India. But I remember each time their names were spoken it was with great regard. I was eager to hear more about these two special people so I traveled to Kathmandu in 2003 to interview some of their Nepali co-workers. The memories they shared with me resounded with praise and respect. They said the Smiths remained faithful through good times and bad. They credited the Smiths with making way for nationals to lead YWAM Nepal, thanks to their immediate trust and inclusion of them. I concluded that it was James and Jean's servant leadership and their love for the Nepali people that produced this lasting fruit in this land of snow-capped mountains.*

*I also interviewed the Smiths, and they continually emphasized that they are just ordinary people carrying out God's calling. They said they made many mistakes, all of which were graciously forgiven by their staff. While the Smiths are ordinary people, God has used them in extraordinary ways. In 2000, the Smiths' time of living in Nepal concluded, but part of their hearts still remains there. They and their four children still live in Asia, and James frequently travels back to Nepal to continue mentoring rising leaders.*

*James Smith was a 25-year-old American working with YWAM Amsterdam in 1981 when God called him to Nepal. He had been asking God for a promise concerning his future, and he was given Romans 15:21, "Those who were not told about him will see, and those who have not heard will understand." James knew this verse was his call to the unreached, and he connected it to his burden for Nepal. After months of waiting, he finally set his feet on Nepali soil in January 1983. Immediately, his heart was captivated by the country and its people. Four months later, he returned to Holland to marry his Dutch fiancé, Jean, and in September they moved to Kathmandu.*

*In my interview with the Smiths, James told me of a statement he once heard someone else say, but became for him something which strongly guided his work in Nepal through the years. The statement was, "My burning desire is to go to the gates of hell, set up camps, and rescue people there." Here is the story of YWAM Nepal's beginning days in the words of James Smith.*

---

# A High Calling

The weathered face of an old man appeared to me in a vision. He hugged a thin shawl around his chest. Then I heard the Lord say, "One day you will meet this man, and he will be very instrumental." God never told me what the man would be instrumental in doing. When the vision was gone, I felt led to open a map of Nepal. My eyes were drawn to three names: Chainpur, Dingla, and Num. These three villages formed a triangle in the east of Nepal near Mount Everest. I sensed somehow these villages were connected to my vision of the old man, but I did not understand what it all meant yet.

From that point on my thirst for information about Nepal grew. Anytime a team returned from there, I eagerly listened to their stories. Nepal offered an expansive task of evangelism, and I knew my taste for spiritual challenge and adventure would be met in this small, mountainous country. I shared the calling with my leaders in Amsterdam, and they freely released me to go.

None of us knew that at the same time Elisabeth Baumann and Judy Sproats were being released by Kalafi Moala in Honolulu to pioneer YWAM Nepal. When I met them in Nepal and heard their vision, it underscored my belief that this was God's time for Nepal. Several months later, when my wife Jean and I returned to Kathmandu as newlyweds, we shared a flat with Elisabeth. Our friendship grew as the three of us spent many hours praying and worshipping together. As we got to know people, we conducted Bible studies for interested Nepalis. Breaking the spiritual ground here required much perseverance and determination.

Because Jean and I sensed we were going to be in Nepal many years, we wanted to get to know the rest of the YWAM family in South Asia, many of whom had come out of Honolulu. We decided that the quickest way to build these relationship was to join the staff of the October 1984 DTS in Uluberia. Through the school we gained many new friendships, and following the lecture phase, we took our mixed team of Nepalis, Indians, Americans, Dutch, Singaporean, Bangladeshi, and Swiss, back to Nepal for an outreach trek. We knew there were Christians living in outlying villages who yearned for more teaching, and our goal was to trek many miles over mountain trails to bring in resources, such as Bibles, and to put on puppet shows as a way to attract crowds and do evangelism.

One day we were packing up our puppets to leave for the next village when we saw two policemen approaching. "Where are your trekking permits?" they asked gruffly. We figured it was only a routine check so we handed over our permits.

"Follow us!" one of the policemen demanded after glancing through our permits.

Our team of nine along with our six porters proceeded to follow them, walking along the narrow trail with little conversation. The policemen never told us where they were taking us. They watched us carefully, leaving no room for anyone to separate from the group. At the end of that day, we stopped at a small empty lodge with a mud floor. They ordered us inside. When the doors shut behind us, and the bolt lock clicked into place, our suspicions were confirmed.

We were under arrest!

Early the next morning, the police let us out to begin another day of walking. Our journey ended later that day when we arrived in a small town. One policeman went inside to announce our arrival and the other remained with us on the street. I discreetly took one of our Nepali porters aside, gave him money and told him to seek help for us in Kathmandu. The police had not done an official count so they never questioned the porter's absence.

When the other policeman returned, we were led inside the jailhouse and our now 14-member team was squeezed into a 3.6 x 2.7 meter cell. All we could do was pray, for none of us had any idea how long we would be in this dark and dirty cell.

The next day we were handcuffed and marched down the street to the courthouse. For my Nepali and Indian teammates, this walk through the town was an incredible humiliation. Typically, foreigners who get in trouble in Nepal are deported, but we soon learned that we were facing a criminal charge — attempting to convert Nepalis to Christianity. When we got back to the cell, we found that our bags had been searched. Clothes and other belongings were scattered around the floor, including diaries in which some of us recorded our joy over the people we had seen commit their lives to the Lord. We panicked at the thought of the guards having access to this evidence, but somehow they had overlooked this information. We hurriedly tore out the incriminating pages and stuffed them inside our clothing. Whenever we went outside to use the bathroom, we dug holes in the ground and buried the evidence there.

The conditions of the jail were rough, but we were treated well by the guards. If we gave them money, they would buy eggs and boil them for us. At one point, they gave only the foreigners food. But we refused to eat until the food was divided equally between all the prisoners.

Not many days after we had been in the jail, the Nepalis on the team were escorted to an upstairs room. The self-appointed lawyer for them said they would have to thumbprint a pre-prepared statement, threatening to beat them if they refused. Every one of them gave their thumbprints, only finding out later that the papers declared them guilty of converting from Hinduism to Christianity, a "crime" punishable by a one-year prison sentence. They were also charged with preaching the Gospel, a charge carrying the same six-year sentence we foreigners were facing.

On the same day we were brought before a lawyer whom we were told would advocate for us. Warmed at this show of justice, we gave him our stories, laying out for him in detail what we were doing. As it turned out, he was the prosecuting attorney and used our innocently-told stories against us.

We had no way to contact anyone for help, and as the days passed, we became concerned that no one in Kathmandu was aware of our plight. As Elisabeth told me later, on the ninth day of our arrest she walked over to the small window in our cell, desperate for a positive breakthrough in our case. Looking at the sky through the cell's small window, she prayed, "God, please help us." Within five minutes, a representative of the American Consulate arrived to plead for our case.

With great excitement, we realized our porter had made it through. The porter had been walking through Kathmandu, not knowing where to go, as this was his first time in the city. A lady who had been in his village ten years ago recognized him! He told her the story and she immediately contacted Dilaram, a ministry we worked closely with. Some may say it was pure coincidence, but looking back we see God's hand in it all. It happened that the very next morning, the senior leader of Dilaram was scheduled to have lunch with the American representative to Nepal! When he heard of our predicament, the American Ambassador called the Consulate and immediately assigned someone to our case. This representative came, along with a talented lawyer from Kathmandu to advocate for us. Although the representative came specifically for the Americans, he played an influential hand in everyone's release.

The day the lawyer arrived, we were released on bail, but the charges were not dropped. Every six weeks, we had to return to the court and sign the *tariq*[7] to verify we had not left the country. The greater miracle of our case was the international attention it brought to Nepal. Soon after our release, a delegation came out and documented cases of human right abuse. Nepal is a signature to the UN's human rights agreement. With their evidence, the delegation put tremendous pressure on the Nepali government and escalated the issue of religious freedom in Nepal. Many Nepali Christians were thrilled because it called their government to accountability. Eventually, every single one of us were acquitted, but each one of us remained committed to the very task that we had been accused for.

After our release, we immediately threw ourselves back into the work. Being in jail had only increased our resolve to do what we believed God had called us to. It had been our desire for some time to start a DTS and now seemed as good a time as any. We saw the DTS was a step toward seeing Nepalis trained and released into leadership. Others thought we were crazy. One senior Christian leader in Nepal approached us, telling us it was irrational to run a DTS because the court case had made us known to the authorities.

Not wanting to ignore his counsel, Jean, Georgina, Elisabeth and I went before the Lord to make sure He had told us to run the DTS. What He replied could not have been clearer. His answer came through Isaiah 52:6, "It is I who foretold it. Yes, it is I."

Not long before the students were due to arrive, the four of us gathered together. In a small circle, we prayed together for the upcoming DTS. With my eyes closed, in front of me I saw a map of the Himalayan region. Out of Kathmandu, bright laser beams shot north toward Tibet, eastward toward Bhutan, west toward North India and Pakistan. When they landed there, they bounced and dispersed further. The lights had gone out from Nepal reaching out into the Tibetan and Buddhist world, and beyond.

Up until now, our vision was confined to Nepal and its people. The Lord was stretching our vision further into the outer regions of the Himalayas and into the Tibetan and Buddhist world. We were serving the God of the impossible. Even though we could only manage to take it one day at a time, an overwhelming sense of joyous emotion filled us all. It was a larger vision, but we were ready. All at once, we started to praise God in loud voices. Around the room were declarations of, "Yes Lord, we will take it." "We will look beyond the borders of Nepal." "We will step out." One of the defining scriptures for that time was Isaiah 45:1-3:

> THIS IS WHAT THE LORD SAYS TO HIS ANOINTED, TO CYRUS, WHOSE
> RIGHT HAND I TAKE HOLD OF TO SUBDUE NATIONS BEFORE HIM AND TO
> STRIP KINGS OF THEIR ARMOR, TO OPEN DOORS BEFORE HIM SO THAT
> GATES WILL NOT BE SHUT: I WILL GO BEFORE YOU AND WILL LEVEL THE
> MOUNTAINS, I WILL BREAK DOWN GATES OF BRONZE AND CUT THROUGH
> BARS OF IRON. I WILL GIVE YOU THE TREASURES OF DARKNESS, RICHES
> STORED IN SECRET PLACES, SO THAT YOU MAY KNOW THAT I AM THE
> LORD, THE GOD OF ISRAEL, WHO SUMMONS YOU BY NAME.

God continued to challenge and nurture us. As staff, we sometimes were unsure what we were doing, and took it one day at a time. There were times of discouragement because of the restrictions we lived under, but we were thankful that our spoken Nepali was improving and our communication more effective. As I looked at the progress of YWAM India, it seemed initially we were moving at a much slower rate. God showed us that He was taking us down a different path, one tailored to the needs of the Nepalis.

In those days, we did our best to minimize any sense of separation between us as foreigners and Nepalis. We ate the same food; we experienced the same struggles; we prayed together for the most basic needs; we shared in our triumphs and in our distress. We were all on the same ground together, and it wasn't long before the Nepalis believed with their hearts that God was the same no matter what culture He was represented in.

Years later, I was given the opportunity to finally trek to Chainpur, Dingla, and Num, the three villages I was led to in my vision back in Amsterdam. As we prepared for this long and dangerous trek, I was excited to see what God had in store for us there. I couldn't have imagined the impact this trek would have.

Our four-member team first took a small 20-seater prop plane to Tumlingtar in eastern Nepal, where we would begin our long journey on foot. Traveling with me were Ann Mosler, a young woman from America who had been with us for a couple of years; Moti Sudemba, a dear Nepali woman with incredible determination and a gentle spirit; and a faithful staff named Prem. His home village was near Chainpur, our last stop. If lines were drawn between each place, these three villages formed a triangle, with Num at the top. Chainpur was across a deep river valley from Dingla.

After four days of trekking, we reached Chainpur. Along the way we met countless numbers of people, many eager to chat with us. A trek into Nepal's mountains is filled not only with beautiful scenery but also frequent interaction with Nepalis who live along the trails. Trekkers are the country's unofficial news-carriers. As trekkers approach, villagers come out to inquire of news from villages passed on the trail, and whether you had eaten. If you haven't eaten, they will gladly feed you, sometimes sacrificing their own meal so you may eat. With half of our four-member team being foreign, our white skin was another attraction for the villagers. Although we were relatively close to Mount Everest, we were not on a tourist route. To reach Mount Everest, you would have to head north. We were heading eastward.

On the day we left, I rose early while the sun was still rising. Above our campsite, I made my way up to a high ridge overlooking Chainpur. The morning air was crisp, and the sun cast a golden glow over the small huts of Chainpur where smoke was rising from the cook fires of villagers preparing their morning tea.

I had walked up the ridge to spend time alone with my Lord, to seek His face in this quiet place. The one thing I asked for that morning was for someone to share the Gospel with. Not five minutes later, footsteps and a stick tapped behind me. An old man wrapped in a shawl walked slowly toward me. I did not recognize him as anyone I had met in the village. He came to stand beside me, and we began to talk. He spoke a tribal language, but we were able to hold a conversation in Nepali. I told him about the love of Jesus and read to him some verses from my Bible.

When I told the man I needed to be leaving, his words cut me to the heart. "You just told me about this God, and now you're leaving. No one in this village knows about this God. I cannot read your book [Bible]. There is no book to tell us what we must do."

As our team walked single file down the narrow path later that morning, the words of this man returned to me. A heaviness settled upon my heart, and sobs rose within my throat. I heard the Holy

Spirit say to me, *THAT IS THE WAY 90% OF THE PEOPLE ARE. HOW ARE THEY TO KNOW ME UNLESS SOMEONE ACTUALLY LIVES AND WALKS AMONG THEM?* During our time on the trail, we had not met a single person who knew or heard of the name Jesus. The old man's words challenged my approach to evangelism. We couldn't go from village to village, share the Gospel and then leave. These people had no resources to fall back onto. They needed another to walk with them, to show them the way, to be a living example to them. With tears partially blinding the way ahead, I cried out for the many unreached Nepalis, for new sets of pioneers who would live in the villages to fill the need expressed by the old man. It would have to be Nepalis. I knew I couldn't be the answer to my own prayer. My white skin made me too visible to authorities, and initially would mark me as a source of money. If Nepalis lived and worked in these villages, they would be God's shining light to these unreached people.

I hadn't recognized it when he was staring me in the face, but later I realized I had seen the old man's face before. His was the face in my vision in Amsterdam. The vision had now come full-circle. It was an exciting revelation, and I felt I had arrived on the threshold of God's incredible plan for Nepal.

The words the old man left me with was the Macedonian call for us in Nepal. As I shared with our small staff, we knew God had clearly given us His word. We were ready to make the new sacrifices necessary to answer the call.

I returned from the trek, more determined than before to release Nepalis into church planting. I looked at our workers and was excited about what God had in store for them. Our Macedonian call did entail a certain danger, because of Nepal's stringent religious laws. But sacrifice was an inherent value in the Nepali culture. Nepali Christians already knew what it meant to count the cost and found it was worth risking their safety. God continued to perform miracles, provided for us and lavished His love on us. As they experienced God's fatherly care toward them, the Nepalis boldly stepped out in faith. Pokhara was the second base to be pioneered after Kathmandu. This was started by an American couple, and Pokhara is the first property to be bought in all of YWAM South Asia. YWAM Pokhara was initiated out of a strong vision to be a training and sending out place for national school leaders. Some years after that, one of our Indian staff approached me and said, "I feel God is calling me to start YWAM in Dharan [east Nepal]." There was an overwhelming joy in my heart when I heard those words. I had been encouraging them many times, and pushing them out. But when this worker came to me out of his own initiative, I thought I would explode with joy. He began the YWAM work, with four other men, on a thick plank of faith and a thin sliver of finances. He had absolutely no foreign backing to fall back upon, but that didn't matter. He had a large measure of faith and God blessed that, greatly multiplying his faith.

Our growth was especially remarkable in light of Nepal's restrictions on religious activities and the discouraging bouts of sickness we suffered. Police would often stand across the street from our house, keeping watch on us, hoping to catch us in some offence. Meanwhile, I frequently battled sickness — not just your usual colds and fevers, but Typhoid, TB, and constant diarrhea that left me weak. At times, the combination of all these struggles tempted us to give up, but it was only through the tremendous spiritual strength, grace, and the dedication of our Nepali and Indian workers that we continued to grow.

Despite these various struggles, the Lord confirmed we were in the right place. There were moments when we could see clearly the way God was moving, and other times we could barely see at all. During one DTS, I became extremely ill and was unable to leave my bed. It was my turn to teach, but I could not even stand up. I called Moti and Kishor (a faithful Nepali staff member) to my room. While they pulled up two chairs, I told them what I had planned to speak on. Then they went downstairs to the lecture hall, delivering to the students exactly what I had told them. They were so willing and proved themselves very capable.

I remained in bed for one month, tied down by circumstances beyond my control. There was nothing but for the others to take control. Back then, I didn't see my sickness as something God placed in order for the Nepali leadership to rise up. But it certainly reinforced the testimony to all of us that God's grace was with us in everything we went through.

During one sickness in 1986, I had lost 18 kilograms and was down to 54 kgs (118 pounds). The doctors in Nepal could do nothing more for me and ordered my evacuation. As my wife Jean is a trained nurse, she was able to leave the country with me as my personal nurse. We were flown to Holland where I received perhaps was the most devastating sentence of my life. After reviewing my case, the doctor said, "You cannot return to Nepal." I had been expecting this, but when the words were audibly spoken, it was if my heart stopped beating. But Jean and I prayed and we both felt we were to return to Nepal. Of course, people thought we were being careless and foolish. Both sets of our parents were understandably concerned with our decision, but gradually their hearts changed. The International YWAM Council told me I could return to Nepal for a six month trial period, and both Jean and I agreed to this. I preferred to live a shorter life and be in the will of God rather than to live a longer and supposedly safer life in the West. I was ready to die in Nepal. Those six months I spent in Nepal were the best six months of my life. Of course I didn't die! I believe sickness was just another method the enemy used to try and scare me out of Nepal.

We've had a fairly steady growth throughout the years. By conducting our schools in Nepali, we have reached more levels of society. Because the schools were conducted in the local language, we were able to recruit people immediately. The incredible faithfulness and love of our Nepali and Indian staff gave us the strength to remain despite all our struggles. The Nepali staff have really been the pillars which held up the work all these years. Soon after we began the DTS, Nepali workers were released into leadership positions, and today they are the majority in leadership nationwide.

When I think back on those days, it seems it was all so different back then. Perhaps much of the spirit of those times had to do with our youthfulness. To sit back and do nothing wasn't an option. All of us had a burning desire to share with others what Jesus had given us. We didn't care what the cost was. We were willing to be seen as stupid. We were willing to make mistakes, and that we certainly did.

I had an unquenchable hunger for more of what God had in

store. Lying on the floor during prayer times, I would cry out. I cried out for God's strength for all of us. Because I realized how weak we were, I realized how little we could do unless we had Him with us. I also cried out for the places that hadn't been reached by His love yet. It was like there was this fire for the lost inside of us that couldn't be quenched. We could never be content with what had been accomplished. We had to constantly keep moving one step forward.

5

# Building with
# Blind Faith and Commitment

*T**he door opened into our tiny room at the YWAM base in Chennai, India, and my daddy walked in. "Well, I had a good time counseling with one of the boys from my flock group[8]," he said, shutting the door behind him. "Sorry that took so long."*

*When he returned, I had been sitting in my mom's lap, listening to her read a story. Now I was bounding toward him with pleading eyes. "Can we finish the story? I want to hear what happened with Bobby and Billy."*

*"I'll try and remember it." He scratched his head and closed his eyes, pondering where he had left off. Only 30 minutes earlier he had walked out of that door, to answer yet another call for help on the YWAM Chennai base.*

*This one room at the base was ours. The rest of the house belonged to whatever number of people happened to be living with us at the time. Because we were a family, and the only family* there, we were the least cramped of anybody. The roof above had been converted into a boys' dorm, by erecting a coconut-thatched roof. The balcony across from us became a guest room simply by attaching a thatched roof and blinds. Down below were two small rooms and a hall. The hall was used for lectures during the day and at night was a sleeping area when needed.

Dad pulled me into his lap and continued our story.

"Bobby reached the top of the hill. He could see trees all around him. All of a sudden…"

KNOCK, KNOCK

Ignoring the knock momentarily, he continued, "All of a sudden, a huge bird flew above him."

Somebody was here again!

"We'll finish this, I promise," he said to me, closing the book. "I'll get the door," he said, seeing that my mom was busy feeding my sister.

"I will be there in five minutes," I heard him say to the person at the door. The door closed and he came and continued the story. When it was finished, he left. Sometimes both my parents were called. Sometimes they took us with them, sometimes they grabbed someone to watch us while they left to take care of the problem.

With a mature hindsight, I now understand why the line was permeable between our family and ministry life. My parents had an unwavering commitment to this community. There was no other living option. My mother did her best to make that one room our home for the time we lived there. But that door was the problem. We could not prevent those knocks on the door. My parents had come to India to serve, and serve they did! Sometimes dad was summoned to fix problems like broken toilets and doors, but more often it was because someone needed counseling. He also walked out that door regularly to meet with pastors or to pick up visitors.

God blessed our family with a tremendous amount of patience and grace during that time, but the demands of the ministry were straining our home life. One guest speaker observed the number of interruptions our family received in a day, and decided to visit our room himself. His knock on our door was the best one we ever received. He exhorted us to move into our own place, to separate our ministry and family life. His concerns voiced my parent's worries.

Nine months later, we found our own house and moved out. It was only two houses around the corner, but it was our very own place! My sister and I even had our own room. Although we still received knocks at our door, they were becoming less frequent. Our home was coming closer to the definition of a family sanctuary.

Even though this was my family's particular experience, the struggles are ones shared by other missionary families. For us, moving out didn't mean abandoning our community life, but rather trying to pull together our own family.

As I look back as an adult, I admire my dad and mom's selfless lifestyle. But as a five-year-old, it was hard to be unselfish and release my father to do what God called him to. I desperately desired stability in my environment. I wanted that to be my parents. Ultimately, I had to release my family, and fully grasp the realization that God was the one unchanging element in my constantly changing world.

While my father was away from our family, he went through struggles of his own. His commitment to his vision of seeing YWAM established in Chennai caused him to spend hours networking with pastors in the city, leading schools and serving the countless needs of the base. In my child's worldview, I had no idea what battles he was fighting. I only knew that I missed him terribly. Our closeness as a family amplified his absences in my mind.

Interestingly, my dad endured similar challenges as a youth. He grew up in the Chicago area where his father was a church planter. He decided early on that he wanted no part of Christian service work. But in his early 20s he fully committed his life to Jesus, and his life goals changed. In 1975, he attended YWAM's School of Evangelism in Lausanne, Switzerland. Following the school, he planned to return to America to get a degree in forestry, but God had different plans. In Switzerland, it seemed that every *intercessors' group Tim was in prayed for India. He eventually joined a prayer team that traveled overland from Switzerland to India. Karol Meidal was on this team and they quickly became friends, sharing a common call to India.*

*They married in 1977 and settled in Urbana, Illinois. This university town is significant in that every three years it hosts the Urbana Missions Conference, which attracts about 20,000 college students interested in missions as a career. My dad attended the 1979 Urbana conference and heard Billy Graham give a compelling message on the Lordship of Jesus Christ. While listening to it, dad saw clearly the map of India, which he took as strong confirmation to return there. In January 1983, he did just that. My parents moved our young family and seven others from YWAM Honolulu to Chennai to pioneer the work of South India. My dad's heart has always been for urban ministries, and he has imparted this vision throughout the nation. Over the past two decades, he has resigned from various roles to allow an Indian to step into his position. My parents remain in India today where he mentors upcoming leaders in his role as YWAM's International Urban Missions Director. Here is the story of their pioneering work in Tim Svoboda's words.*

# The Importance of Commitment

I folded my map, and started to get off the bus. I nodded my head in gratitude at my seatmate, without whose help I might have missed my stop.

"Excuse me." I yelled over the noisy chatter and horns blasting. No one seemed to hear me. I shouted louder. It made no difference. The bus was slowing down. The crowd on the bus didn't exactly move to let me make my way to the door. I tried to see how others were getting off. People pushed others aside, using their bags, their hands, anything to get to the doors. I did the same, making a forceful push forward with my shoulder, eventually landing at the bottom steps of the door. The conductor's whistle blew and the bus finally stopped. Waiting was a crowd that seemed larger than the one leaving the bus. Glad that I wouldn't be there for the tighter squeeze, I jumped off.

I walked down the road, sweat collecting where my shirt was tucked into my trousers, looking for a church. I wasn't sure where I was going but knew the church was in this area. I scanned my eyes over the small buildings, looking for a spire or a cross, something resembling a church. After several minutes, I found one and made my way there through the many small streets.

"Tim Sapota!" I turned to see who had called my name. My last name had always been a hard one for people to say. Here in India, I heard even more variations on it! A man in dark brown trousers and a neatly ironed white cotton shirt was walking toward me.

I greeted him, saying, "Praise the Lord, Pastor," pressing my palms together and raising them to my chest.

"Praise the Lord," he replied. "It was so nice to see you at the meeting the other night."

I had talked to him a little about YWAM and had expressed a desire to share more with him.

"Come to my office. We can talk there."

As I sat down on the cane-wicker chair in his office, we talked a little about our families and how I was finding my time in India. Leaning back in his seat, the silver tumbler of tea in his hand, the pastor asked, "So tell me what it is you want to do here? What was this organization you were telling me about the other day?"

I poured out to him my vision for YWAM in India.

"Do you really think people will be willing to work with YWAM if there is no salary? That won't work here in India. It is a child's duty to support his parents when able to. You cannot expect them to work for free," he responded.

I bowed my head in frustration. It seemed I continually came up against this wall of objection over the past year.

"Yes, I know. I realize this. But I have seen God continuously provide for me. My biggest fear that held me back from coming to India was my two young daughters. I feared that I would not be able to provide for them. But everyday I have seen God provide food and other needs for our family."

"Well, Tim, people here look for jobs that can help them support their families and working a paying job is very important."

I knew what he was really saying behind his words. I also understood that when you are concerned with paying your bills regularly and are working a full-time job, it is hard to quit that lifestyle and believe the money will simply be handed to you. Living by faith was a hard concept to convince anyone of, not only in India, but almost anywhere in the world. I explained the concept to the pastor. Besides being the God of this Universe, God was also our Heavenly Father and He would provide for us when we were obedient to His call upon our lives. I realized as a foreigner I gave off the impression of having financial backing from my country, something Indians do not have. I hoped there was a way to assure the Christian community here that we were all on the same ground when it came to faith in God. Living by faith was a concept many pastors were familiar with. They received a minimal or scant salary and depending on God for their support was normal. But for them to ask young members of their congregation, who were expected to provide for their families, to live on the same principle was a monumental task.

I hoped that in time our lives would be an example, and people would see God's faithfulness in our lives and know with certainty God would be just as faithful to them. I understood where they were coming from. The only way I could convince them was through my actions and living out my faith daily.

Even though I faced this attitude regularly, they were still exceedingly warm toward me. They were interested in me, in my family, in how we liked living in their country.

This pastor's comment and many others came out of the current political situation in India. We arrived 28 years after the British left India, but their influence remained strong. Some were pushing for a complete nationalization of India, and in 1975 Prime Minister Indira Gandhi placed India under emergency rule. She ordered all foreign businesses to leave the country and nationalization efforts began. The campaign "Be Indian, Buy Indian," aimed to rid India of foreign products and enable her to stand on her own strength.

Although not the intention of the government, this act catalyzed indigenous Indian missions.

Our SOE team from Switzerland arrived in India soon after emergency rule was declared. We never should have been able to enter the country, but we did because God's hand was clearly upon us. Prayer covered each step of the way, and it was evident. It had taken us 40 days to drive our two vehicles from Lausanne to India with numerous stops along the way. We traveled across perilous areas of Eastern Europe, the Middle East and Asia, but nothing prepared us for India.

We had no concrete plan for our time there. We came simply because God had called us, and we spent much of our time praying over the nation. On my own initiative, I passed out tracts and shared the Gospel with people on the streets. After two months, my team members returned to their home countries. I stayed on for four months, doing various jobs. I worked with a crusade team traveling around the country and then with an organization called Dilaram, which ministers to Western drug addicts in India and Nepal. The most important lesson I learned during that time was commitment. I saw that without commitment, nothing substantial could be done in India. Although our 1975 team never put down physical roots in the country, I believe we laid a foundation for YWAM India through intercession. Spiritually speaking, that team put the first shovel into the soil of the land, going from city to city and paving the way for future workers to come through our prayers.

My wife and I are the only ones from that team who returned to India, although our team leader Paul Hawkins has kept his heart tied to the nation in many ways. While he hasn't settled down here, he has visited the country many times and has given of his time and wisdom in countless ways to see YWAM India grow.

When I returned in 1983, few foreigners remained in the nation. Indians agreed with their government, and rightly so, that Indians needed to be in charge of their own affairs. Indian Christians also were confident that missions could continue without the help of foreigners. I was glad to see this independence. Yet, I also knew beyond a doubt that I had been called to India to establish YWAM, and had to follow that call despite my "foreignness." My vision was also for seeing nationals leading the ministry, and I believed that one day it would be a reality. Meanwhile, the feeling that I, as a foreigner, could not do much here was discouraging.

After my visit with the pastor, I stopped in Kolkata to visit Mark Buntain. I had met him for the first time in 1975 during our SOE team's visit to Kolkata, where we attended his church on Sundays. He was interested in what we were doing, and I was amazed at the work he had established. To me, he was a great pioneer of Christian ministries in India and had a heart for Kolkata and West Bengal. I hoped that in my visits with him and to his work, I would learn something which would benefit YWAM India.

Before Steve Cochrane had moved the YWAM base out to Uluberia, he had spent much of his time in Kolkata, networking with other pastors and Christian leaders. Mark Buntain was one of the people he contacted, and they developed a healthy partnership. Mark referred many people into our DTSes.

Mark Buntain and his wife Huldah, came to Kolkata in October 1954 to serve for a year. They remained many years past their intended stay and shaped a ministry that has touched thousands of lives. Out of a simple vision, they founded a church, which today has a staff of 19 pastors and services are conducted in eight Indian languages. In 1977, a 200-bed hospital was completed, which treats 150,000 people annually. Many of the hospital's services are offered free of charge.

We spent some time walking through the Buntains' hospital, church, and their other ministries. The time here was over, but I left feeling empowered. I was encouraged that I had not come to India in vain.

The hospital gates closed behind us. We turned around for a last glance. As we stood outside those gates, I said to my friend, "Man, isn't this incredible?"

He turned to me and in all seriousness said, "Yes, you can do the same thing too if you stay for 30 years."

Those words struck me hard. Here, I had spent a day feeling empowered, and I was ready to return to Chennai and pour more of myself into what we were doing there. Thirty five years! Mark

Buntain had been here that long. I had no idea how long I would remain in India, but I never thought it could be as long as thirty years. I had only been here for a year now, and had come up against so many walls.

As I looked in my Indian brother's eyes, the truth took a defined shape. I saw the need for a deeper commitment. The Indians had to know we were here to stay, that we were committed to them, so they could take full leadership.

I returned to Chennai, with a stronger resolve and a more realistic picture of the future. It was no longer filled with idealism and vagueness. Through this newly opened window, I saw a great need for Indian workers. As a foreigner, the option of returning to the US when things got too hard was always there. But, my vision was for a partnership between the Indians and foreigners, one where we would learn from each other. In my honest Indian brother's statement, he shined a light onto the next step. He showed me that above all, we needed to be committed wholeheartedly to what we had set out to do.

# 6

# Deepening the
# Bonds of Our Foundation

*In October of 1984 YWAM leaders called their second South Asia staff conference. We gathered at a beach resort in Mahabalipuram, about an hour south of Chennai. Since most of the staff at the time were young singles, my sister Ana and I were the only children to attend. While our parents were in meetings, we often were out playing with Indian children we met at the resort's playground.*

*Unlike our parents, we did not have a strong sense of being foreign. When we approached other children on the playground we didn't worry about what they would think of us or about cultural differences. To us they were just possible playmates, kids with whom we could have contests with on the swings. I remember times as a child, playing with Indian children, thinking I was just like them. Then I would look down at myself and see my white hands and feet. My reaction was usually "oh" and a brief moment of puzzlement. Because I was a child, I didn't think too long about it and carried on with my games. I sometimes miss the feeling of carefree abandonment I had at that time.*

*By contrast, my parents and the other foreign YWAM staff fought inward battles every day over their ways of thinking and behaving. Cultural differences required them to develop new life patterns. Some changes were petty details; others were major shifts. Sometimes these differences caused friction, but they also caused them to look more closely at their own culture. They learned to sift out the negatives, retain the positives and to learn from other cultures. Ultimately, these struggles bonded together the foreign and Indian YWAMers, as the love of God overshadowed their differences. One long-term YWAMer in India likened these budding relationships to that of Apostle Paul and the young man he took into his care, Timothy.*

*At the Mahabalipuram conference of 1984 the Holy Spirit deepened the bond of brotherhood between the foreign and national staff in YWAM South Asia through one radical act of love and humility. The servant leadership model of Jesus was experienced anew by the foreigners and nationals alike as they learned to work together, paving the way for a new level of understanding and acceptance.*

*I was too young then to take in what happened at the time. But when I heard this story years later from Wendy (Mahbert) Paul, I understood just how critical this breakthrough was for us as a mission in South Asia. Wendy herself played a key role in the event, and she was one of God's gifts to YWAM in those early days. As a Nepali and having grown up in North India, she was an invaluable cultural asset to the teams and became a strong leader. She is presently serving in Central Asia in missions along with her husband, David Paul, and their two children.*

*In her interview, Wendy described how God led her into YWAM as a teenager. For years after the death of her father, she had rejected God. She told me she felt that if God truly loved her, he would not have let her father die. Then one day, after an awful time at school, she came home and started shouting at God:*

*"If you are God, then you've got to show yourself to me now or that's it!"*

*Exhausted, she fell asleep. When she woke up, a strange light shone throughout the room. Sensing God's presence, she knelt beside her bed and gave her heart to Jesus. That night, as years of pain and bitterness washed away, Wendy also made a commitment to go into missions. So a short time later, when a YWAMer came to her church in Sikkim, she took one of his DTS application forms. In January 1982, she made her way by faith to the DTS in Singapore. Nine months later, she joined Steve Cochrane and his team in Kolkata. Their team was at the Mahabalipuram conference, and here in Wendy's own words is a description of what happened.*

---

# In the Steps of Jesus

We were finally here, after two long days on the train from Kolkata. When everyone arrived at the staff conference, we would be a total of 90, including several YWAM leaders from overseas. That number had grown since our first conference in Nepal, but most of the staff were still foreigners. As we checked in, the atmosphere felt like the arrival of the monsoons after a scorching summer. People greeted each other as if they hadn't seen each other for many years. Tears shed quickly, and laughter rang freely. I marveled at how these people – so different from me in various ways – had become my second family.

I thought back to my first experiences as a staff member. Every time we went to churches to spread the word about YWAM, I stuck out sorely, for two reasons — one because I wasn't a foreigner, and two because all of them towered above me in height. There were many challenging times, but I admired these young foreigners' commitment to India and Nepal. As they talked, their love for God and passion for the nation was evident in each word they spoke. Through our fellowship, my respect for them deepened. Despite our friendship, working together wasn't always easy. We often had very different approaches to our work, and had to learn that one way was not more "wrong" or "right" than the other.

Because of my upbringing, I felt more at ease around the

foreigners than my Indian brothers and sisters. I often found myself serving as a buffer between both groups. At times both sides would ask for the same issue to be addressed, but from two opposite vantage points. Indians asked me to tell the foreign women to cover their ankles. The foreigners asked me to tell the Indian women to cover their midriffs when wearing saris.

Many of us nationals also struggled with YWAM's way of leadership. In most other organizations in India, leaders were highly respected — an excellent value, but in many cases it also led to distance between the leadership and staff level. As we discovered the different life of YWAM, we learned the importance of balancing both worldviews — retaining the respect while also developing friendships with our leaders. The YWAM leaders would share their struggles in front of us – even in front of the students. They ate at the same tables as us, played volleyball games with us, and when we traveled together, they did not ride in a higher class. Many of the nationals were especially surprised to see Steve Cochrane and Tim Svoboda sweeping the lecture hall floors. Although we were initially confused at their humble lifestyle, it eventually created a greater level of respect for them and placed us all on the same ground.

They also changed our view of missions. To us, missionary work was something highly spiritual, such as immersing oneself in Scriptures and evangelism. The other duties of life carried nothing spiritual. But for the first time, we were seeing another dimension of missionary work; serving the Lord also meant cleaning someone's toilet out of love. It brought a new, but assuring balance to our perception of Christian service.

I first saw this during the 1983 DTS in Uluberia where God began softening my own heart. I was on staff, but I was learning right alongside the students. The teachings were real and life-changing. Classroom lessons were put into practice each hour in our community living. YWAM's method of modeling the Christian life in community was something we could understand. Because the countries of South Asia are very much a community culture, I could see that this was the best learning environment for us.

Now our growing community was here in Mahabalipuram,

and we sat for hours together, relating stories of our experiences. Many of us felt it was only within this family we could talk about our struggles of faith and finances. Because YWAM was still so new in the country, the church often misunderstood us. We also felt isolated in other ways. We weren't on the popular tourist route or any "route" in particular. So the presence of those leaders who had been crucial to YWAM's birth in South Asia encouraged us and gave a sense of outside support. There was an excitement as we looked forward to continue to build on our friendships without the limitations of distance.

During that conference, we felt the strong presence of the Lord. It was a time of refreshment. Different ones got up and shared their struggles. For all of us to be there, each one had made sacrifices; each of us had persevered through the hard times, holding tightly onto God's grace. While we all made sacrifices, the foreigner's sacrifice carried a different, (but not heavier) weight to it. They had given up their family and friends and the comfort of their own country to be here. Many of them came here with little to nothing, but gave everything to remain in the country, although there were many tempting times for them to return to the life they had previously known. It wasn't difficult for them to adapt to the externals of the Indian lifestyle, such as eating with their hand and wearing a *pyjama kurta*[9] or a *churidar*[10], but they struggled in understanding the behavior and mindset of the Indian culture. As I heard the words behind their stories, an idea came to me.

This conference would be ending tomorrow, and it seemed to be a perfect time to express our appreciation as Indians toward our foreign co-workers. So I gathered the Indians together to share my idea with them.

"We've all been in YWAM for various amounts of times. I know you've all seen the tremendous commitment of Tim and Karol, Steve, Elisabeth, Brad, David and all the others who came here a couple years ago," All nodded their heads in agreement. "I don't know when we'll all be together like this as a group. While listening to different ones tell their stories, I was impressed with the sacrifices they had made to be here and their commitment to stay. Here's an idea I had of how we can honor them and show them we are standing beside them."

After the final meeting, we would wash the feet of the foreigners. There had been a couple of times when we washed each other's feet to express our love and honor toward each other. We decided to use this same example, but do it as a ministry from us Indians toward our foreign brothers and sisters. We wanted them to know our appreciation and wanted them to know we were just as committed to the vision as they were.

I asked each person to choose who they'd like to honor, making sure each foreign staff was honored. We made plans to gather buckets and towels and place them behind the meeting hall. I designated John Joseph and Ian Liu to lead the time. I felt it was appropriate that as males they lead the meeting.

As I walked to my room through the thick grove of Ashoka trees, the irony of what we were about to do tonight struck me. An act of humility is to touch a person's feet and make yourself lower than them. Feet are considered the dirtiest part of the body. So to wash another's feet is an act of deep honoring toward the other person. I wondered how the others were thinking about this.

During the evening meeting, it was hard to sit still. All I could think about was what was going to follow. Excitement filled me, and I hoped that the Holy Spirit would fill the room. Finally, the meeting finished. People began to rise up out of their chairs.

As planned, John Joseph got out of his chair and walked quickly to the front. "Could everyone sit down, please?" he paused, waiting for them to settle down. "Okay, go do what we planned," looking around the room at our small group. There were confused looks on the faces of the foreigners. I grinned. They had no idea what was ahead.

As the small group left the room, John left with them, saying over his shoulder, "Sorry, this is unplanned, but there is something we would like to do for you. Just wait for a few moments."

I walked out of the room to join the others. The towels were handed out as someone else filled the buckets with water. Gathering in a circle, we said a prayer. Taking one towel and a bucket each, we walked back into the front of the room.

Each of us walked toward our chosen person. Silence hung heavily over the room. Surprise was written on everyone's face. I walked over to Jane Henderson-Cleland. She was the sole foreigner on my women's team called RUTH (Reaching the Unreached Through Homes). I had seen her tears and heard her frustrations with living in India. Underneath all that was a beautiful commitment and sincerity in her heart about what she was doing. I appreciated her honesty and also her servant's heart. As I washed her feet, I thanked God for the opportunity of working alongside her.

Brad and some others tried to get out of their chairs, insisting they should be the ones washing our feet. I smiled at their humility, but watched approvingly as they were made to sit back down and accept the act for what it was. Tears flowed freely around the room. I didn't quite understand what, but sensed God was doing something powerful in this room. After we finished and dried their feet, we prayed together. There was a tangible sense of goodness and love saturating the room.

I gave thanks to God for these wonderful people. They had sacrificed so much to come here. Few of them were prepared. Many of them had a vague picture of what they were to be doing here, but came merely because God called them. I heard sniffs as I prayed and lifted my head. We had reversed the tables on the foreigners. They had come here to serve us, but we wanted to serve them, and this was our chance.

An explanation was due, and I had been the one chosen to do that. I walked to the centre of the room and gazed around for a minute. Steve sat in his chair, his eyebrows knitted together in confusion. I remember my first meeting with this man and his warm welcome. He had greeted me as if I was a long-time family friend and not a stranger. Brad Carr sat hunched over in his chair, his head in his hand. I knew he realized the impact of this night. His sharp shoulder bones poked through his shirt. I laughed silently as I thought of my mother's immediate run to her cooking pot if she saw his state. All of these people, they were young like me. Through the tough times, all of us had learnt together to hang on firmly to the call of God on our lives. It was time to say something, before the silence became uncomfortable.

"I know we shocked you guys with this," I said. Heads bobbed up and down around the room in agreement. "First of all, we want to say thank you. Thank you for answering God's call to come here and serve. Thank you for coming without hesitation." I began to shake my finger mockingly. "And we now know your secrets. You guys weren't prepared, and a lot of you didn't even want to come." With a switch of tone, I said, "Secondly, what just happened here was our way of honoring you for the sacrifice you made to come here, and the commitment you've shown despite the struggles."

Around the room I heard stifled cries and sniffles. A simple act transformed into something powerful. God had truly come down and bonded us together with His love. Things were going to be different from this day forth. We were going to march forward, inseparable by strong bonds of love, and yet still celebrate each other's differences.

"We love you guys." I said with full sincerity. "I've sensed something has changed in this room tonight. The Lord has really met us here. I know each of us will be returning carrying something special in our hearts and a stronger bonding of relationship with each other."

*WHEN HE HAD FINISHED WASHING THEIR FEET, HE PUT ON HIS CLOTHES AND RETURNED TO HIS PLACE. "DO YOU UNDERSTAND WHAT I HAVE DONE FOR YOU?" HE ASKED THEM. "YOU CALL ME 'TEACHER' AND RIGHTLY SO, FOR THAT IS WHAT I AM. NOW THAT I, YOUR LORD AND TEACHER, HAVE WASHED YOUR FEET, YOU ALSO SHOULD WASH ONE ANOTHER'S FEET. I HAVE SET YOU AN EXAMPLE THAT YOU SHOULD DO AS I HAVE DONE FOR YOU. I TELL YOU THE TRUTH, NO SERVANT IS GREATER THAN HIS MASTER, NOR IS A MESSENGER GREATER THAN THE ONE WHO SENT HIM. NOW THAT YOU KNOW THESE THINGS, YOU WILL BE BLESSED IF YOU DO THEM (JOHN 13:12-17).*

**7**

# A Bittersweet Lesson and Growth

The 1984 Mahabalipuram conference marked an important milestone in YWAM South Asia's history. It not only strengthened bonds between individuals, it forged a new spirit of common purpose. Foreign leaders like my father returned with a stronger resolve to release Indian and Nepali nationals into leadership. And the Indian and Nepali nationals returned with a stronger sense of ownership in YWAM and anticipation for the future. But once they left the conference and re-entered their "normal" lives back in Chennai, Kolkata and Kathmandu, this new unity and commitment to expanding the mission were soon put to the test.

God was as concerned about their personal development as He was about YWAM's development. Their youthful stamina and the excitement of pioneering could only carry them so far. To grow them individually and corporately, God had to continue working on their character. He used their weaknesses to bring them to a new level of dependence on Him, leading to new breakthroughs in the Spirit for YWAM. God wasn't going to let them forget Who they were working for.

In July of the following year, my dad faced a major test, one that would mould him as well as the work of YWAM Chennai. The base had scheduled a Discipleship Training School and a School of Evangelism to run simultaneously. With the prospect of 60 people living in a three-bedroom house, my dad and his team felt an urgency to find a larger facility. This "crisis" forced a choice of whether he would follow God's principles or bow to his own desires. It was also an endurance test for staff and students as they lived together in cramped conditions.

My dad's personal lesson brought a breakthrough in the Chennai base and a releasing of more Indian workers into leadership positions. Many who were present look back on this time as formative for staff and students alike. Some describe the sense of holiness felt upon walking onto the property. Others remember the patience they were forced to learn due to the circumstances. The following story spans a period of three months. It is Tim Svoboda's own account of the events that tested YWAM Chennai from July to September 1985.

# On the Grinding Stone

At midnight, I completed my seventh prayer walk around the building in Pallavaram, Chennai. "Lord, You know how much we need a place. The students are coming. We can't all live in that three-bedroom house in St. Thomas Mount anymore. I believe You opened up this place for us. We need to see You come through financially. I claim this house for YWAM Chennai in Jesus' name. Amen." My prayers had become more urgent with each round. I walked back to the chest-high, rusted iron gate and left the house, confident God would bless my faith by providing this house for our

45 arriving DTS students and SOE students to live in.

As the base director, I was responsible for finding a house. I had spent many hours searching for a place. I found this house in April, and it seemed perfect. The grounds were spacious and it had facilities suitable for our training. After much negotiation with the landlord, I settled on what seemed a reasonable price and reported it to our base leadership. To my surprise, they didn't feel a complete peace about it. Though I firmly believed this was the house the Lord wanted us to take, I chose not to move ahead. From previous experience, I understood the importance of unity within our leadership team in making any major decision. This certainly fit that description as it involved finances we would need to trust the Lord for.

Though I was tempted to follow my own logic, I was well aware of the three principles the Lord had taught me about making major decisions. First, no decision should ever go against what the Word of God teaches. Secondly if I am making a major decision, as I was in this case, then those who share leadership with me should be in agreement. If even one on the leadership team has a reservation, I need to see that reservation as God's red light saying "no" or yellow light of caution. In listening to other's reservations, God sometimes reveals areas which need further clarification. The third principle is there should be an inner peace sensed when making decisions. Since the Spirit of Christ lives within He will give peace or a sense of disturbance over such decisions, and we need to discern internally what is going on. Having considered these three factors, if even one is out of line then we should not move forward. This is why I submitted to the leadership and did not take the Pallavaram house on my own initiative.

When a pastor from New Zealand visited us, we asked him to pray with us about this house. He felt it was the right place to run the DTS. This time the leadership council felt we should move forward on securing the house.

With their approval, I went to give the landlord the money for the first month's rent. I prayed as I weaved through traffic on my motorbike, but my late-night prayer walks around the building had given me confidence that the landlord wouldn't cause any problems with the rent. As I arrived, I reached a sweaty palm into my trousers pocket making sure the check was still safely there. Then I waited excitedly for the landlord to answer the doorbell. A few moments later, he welcomed me in.

"Sir, we will take this house. I have the first month's payment with me." I said, reaching out to hand over the check.

The landlord put up his hand.

"No need. I have already given this place to another company."

All I could say was "What?"

"Yes. Someone else asked for the house. So I rented it to them instead."

There was nothing else left to say. His rental was final. As I sped away on my motorbike, my mind was haunted with the question of *where is God when you really need Him?* He knew we needed more space. I looked at the coming three months with increasing anxiety.

In just seven days the DTS and SOE would begin, and a visiting team from overseas would arrive. There was not enough time to find another place. Where were we to put everyone? Our house in St. Thomas Mount already was full. We were expecting around 45 students, this would bring us to 60 people in a three-bedroom house!

Seven days later, on the first day of the DTS and the SOE that three-bedroom house was still all we had. The SOE students had their lectures in the driveway, open to the curious eyes of our neighbors, under palm trees and a blazing sun.

I stood in front of the 45 students seated in the hallway. I apologized to them about the tight living conditions and explained what had happened with the house in Pallavaram. With regret I said, "I trusted the Lord, I sought the Lord and we don't have any prospect of additional housing. I don't know what to tell you. I can't explain it. I don't know what to say except let's just worship the Lord right now." I looked at Ian Liu, asking that he lead us.

Ian came up, propped his guitar on his knee and started to sing, "We love you, Lord."

I can't remember a more phenomenal time of worship than that particular moment. We all experienced the presence of God in a powerful way. We prayed for each other, weeping, and crying out to God. Ian continued to sing worship songs while this went on. In our desperation, God touched us in far greater power than before this difficulty began. Many of us had looked at the coming three months in dread, because of the 60 people crammed into one house. But God was showing us that He was working in this situation for our good.

That house in St. Thomas Mount was simply called 8/17 because of its street number. It was situated in a military cantonment area, just off one of Chennai's main roads. This meant a securer water supply, which we really needed that summer. Opposite the house was an empty field, which we put to good use for volleyball games, small groups, and Saturday night coffeehouses. The two bedrooms on the ground floor were used by single female staff and students. Our family lived in the other bedroom on the middle floor, and the guestroom was simply a balcony that we closed in with cane shades. Above us on the flat roof, 30 young men slept under a coconut-thatched covering that we built to convert the roof into a dormitory. On the ground floor was a small sitting room, converted into a bedroom that summer. A further door in this sitting room led to the small lecture hall where our incredible worship time took place. There was also a garage to the side of the house, which we also used for housing. With no wall to separate us, our neighbors heard clearly our worship times and the words of some guest speakers.

During the July DTS and SOE, I remember students rising at unusual hours such as three, four, and five a.m. just so they could take a shower. When we had intercession or base meetings, there was literally no walking space. The hall was filled, as well as the sitting room, the driveway and around the building. Staff listened to lectures from the outside through the windows because there was no space to sit. You had to stay put until the prayer was over, because it was almost impossible to walk around. But through it all we tangibly felt God's grace. A strong peace rested on 8/17 and in each of our hearts. People commented on this as they walked through the gate. It would have been so easy to get frustrated with our living conditions, but we didn't because of the peace and grace we experienced.

Toward the end of the DTS, I called a meeting. Looking out at these dear Indian workers, I exhorted them to take up more leadership roles. But they were hesitant to step up. They wanted career stability, and YWAM could not offer them that. Most enjoyed their experience with the mission but few thought of it as a long-term career option. They were looking beyond YWAM to the time when they would settle into a job with a secure monthly salary.

Financial support created the largest division between foreigners and Indians. As foreigners, we had the security of family and churches in the West that sent us money. But our Indian brothers and sisters did not have this. The notion of supporting missionaries monthly was a foreign concept for the Indian church at the time. Supportive Indian families helped their children out where possible, but it often wasn't enough. Our schools' low retention rate was largely due to this lack of financial support. Students were happy to soak up all the training we gave them, but to continue with YWAM was not something that crossed their minds.

In many ways, the policy of YWAM was the reverse of other mission organizations. Indian believers were used to supporting mission organizations but not individual missionaries. Other organizations raised funds for their projects and workers while YWAM had each worker raise their own support!

My words were failing to reach their hearts. John Joseph, one of our Indian workers stood up, walked to the front and stood beside me. Without waiting he said, "Come on. We can do this. We can't depend on foreigners to support us. That isn't going to work. We have to trust in the Lord." People stood up and began to encourage each other, telling each other their Father would provide. Money wasn't hidden under pillows. Foreigners were not going to support them, but their Father would. An Indian mission leader was with us, and she sat in the room at that meeting, watching in amazement. After the meeting she approached me and said, "Where did you get these people? You may not have buildings or infrastructure but you have quality people!" I felt like I would burst with pride at that point. It was exciting to see these workers going beyond following instructions and taking an active part.

Three months later, the DTS lecture phase was over and the students were gone. The building was strangely quiet. People weren't at every corner. Although my girls missed their playmates, at least they didn't have to be on tiptoes now that lectures were over. During one of my quiet times, the Lord led me to Matthew 14:22-36, which describes when Peter tried to walk on the water. I didn't really understand how the passage applied to me. Looking through a commentary, I saw that Peter had faith, but he also had pride. Peter was the first to take Jesus' invitation to walk on water and the first one to the tomb to make sure Jesus really wasn't there. When Jesus told Peter He was going to wash Peter's feet so he would be united with Jesus, Peter said he should wash all of him, but Jesus said his feet were enough (John 13:7-9).

Peter was a competitive Christian, and God showed me that I was like Peter. I was reminded of the house in Pallavaram and how I was being competitive, and trying to outdo those around me in my devotion to God. Now I understood the reason we didn't get the house was because of my pride. I wanted to show we were better than the Kolkata YWAM centre and had a bigger and better property than them. Like Peter, I had become competitive in my spirituality. Because of my pride, God shut the door. Like with Peter, He allowed me to sink so I could then say, "What you do in my life is more important than what you do through my life."

Sometimes God has to let us sink so He can save us! When Peter boldly stepped out on the water, God let him begin to sink but then saved him. This may not be a popular message in today's success-driven world but Jesus knew that when Peter sank he would not only cry out to be saved but desire a deeper understanding of what made him sink. God lets us sink to the bottom so He can work a deeper miracle in our own hearts, bringing a new revelation of ourselves. This was the position I had found myself in.

It was hard, but I had to repent in front of our community. I had to explain to them that it was my pride and competitive spirit that got in the way of God giving us the place in Pallavaram. But out of this, God had carved something good. Although not easy, the

8/17 crunch brought us closer. Some of our long-term leaders in the country came out of this time. They have gone on to pioneer other YWAM centers around the country and head up our major ministries. I look back now and marvel at that time. God's presence was so real for those three months. Out of my weakness He birthed Indian leaders, some who are still going strong today. Some of those present that day were Richie Kleinman–who has consistently led DTSes over the years; Francis Balla–who helped pioneer the work in Hyderabad; P. Daniel–a key player in the ongoing work in Dharmapuri, South India; and Rose Thomas–a strong woman leader.

Before the DTS started, I had stood on the roof of our 8/17 house looking over the houses in that area. I pointed to various houses and claimed them. When the DTS was over, I reflected on the lessons I had learned. I remembered this time on the roof, and realized how many houses were opening up to us now. Despite my pride, God still honored my faith.

God placed us on the grinding stone for those three months; grinded us and purified us. It was another birthing process. This lesson had to be learned before He could take us to the next level. This next level was seeing our Indian workers released into leadership, confident that their Father would take care of their every need and stepping into all that God had planned for them.

8

# Lessons from Within

*I* *have heard it said that to really understand your own culture you must look at it from the outside. I experienced the truth of this when I left India in 1999 to attend university in America. I was not only outside India, but I was also outside YWAM. Throughout my years at university, I increasingly found myself drawn towards people of different cultures and felt most "at home" within multi-cultural groups. It was here I realized one of the great strengths of the YWAM culture I had grown up in. Diversity is a long-held foundation of YWAM, which in many ways is a microcosm of the global melting pot.*

*Just as there are many values that make up a culture, so are there many values that make up YWAM. These Foundational Values go against long-held cultural perceptions and are taught within YWAM centers across the world. In interviews with many of our national staff, they expressed to me an initial difficulty with these values and then a gradual warm acceptance. One person put it this way, "YWAM cuts across many of the ideas and principles we were brought up with. It is really turning us to Bible principles, not to Indian or Western culture. It brings stability and oneness amongst us because we go through the same struggles." The principles she was referring to include servant leadership, living by faith, and right relationships across barriers of caste, ethnic, gender and cultural backgrounds.*

*Discipleship Training School is where people often get their first introduction to YWAM values and the YWAM lifestyle. One issue students face immediately is that of cross-cultural relationships. The diversity of South Asia heightens this aspect. For example, a student from Mumbai who comes to DTS in Bangalore may find his roommates are from Nepal and the Indian states of Manipur and Punjab.*

*My own DTS in Lausanne, Switzerland bore many similarities to this. We were a small school – just 14 students – but we represented eight nationalities. My roommates were from Australia and South Korea. Most of us were the sole representative from our countries, except for South Korea (which had two) and America (which had five). True to many cross-cultural beginnings, the Americans and South Koreans stuck to their own kind, while the rest of us had none of our own and were forced to reach out. But eventually every heart was opened to other cultures and by the time we began the final preparations for outreach, the team dynamics had really changed. With more culture shock in store during outreach, our relationships were about to become even closer.*

*Richie Kleinman, who has been leading DTS since 1987 in Chennai has seen this story played out in various ways in DTS. "The key thing we've seen is the whole area of forgiveness. They [students] learn to love one another. After every school, the students cry because they're going home. They don't want to go because they have all become so close. They have opened their lives and shared their weaknesses, and it brings bonding."*

*DTS teaches that life is a learning process, and once we think we've learnt all we need to learn, then God immediately reminds us of how much we don't know. Some of the other values which will be explored in this chapter are living by faith, giving up rights, and proper cross-cultural relationships.*

*This chapter will be a different format than the ones that have preceded. This collection of stories showcases the experiences of many of the national workers and how they worked through different aspects of YWAM. It will show their initial impressions of YWAM, and the issues they walked through in their own personal life within the mission.*

*Editorial note: Richie & Cheryl Kleinman are faithful YWAM leaders originally from Kolkata. Both did DTS in 1985, and they were married the following year. In 1986 they moved to Chennai, serving there in various ways. In 1996, Richie took up the position of Chennai DTS Co-ordinator (as Chennai had DTSes running in different parts of the city), and he still serves in this position today. Cheryl has served alongside her husband, teaching in schools, counseling students and assisting in hospitality at the Kottivakam DTS centre in Chennai.*

"India is a nation of many nations. One of the biggest challenges [in DTS] is trying to bring different nations under one roof. What we've seen happen here, only God can do that."

Richie Kleinman speaks from long experience in leading DTSes in India. He knows well the difficulties that arise as a DTS brings in people from many different walks of life to live together in a community setting.

"Every hour of the day, they mingle with each other, whether in the classrooms, during meal times, walking into town to eat a *dosai*[11], practicing skits and songs for outreach or talking together after hours. DTS often brings out the best and the worst in people. Many times, there are cultural clashes and people are challenged to look beyond their stereotypes and comfort zones.

"In one particular DTS, cliques formed. South Indians were seen together, at meals and during their free times. North and Northeastern Indians were a "group." There was little inter-mingling between these groups. A prevailing unspoken rule was if you were from the South you weren't welcome to mingle with the North Indians and vice-versa.

"India's Independence Day was approaching, and our DTS staff had planned a time of intercession for the nation. After the flag raising and singing of the national anthem was finished, a map of India was drawn on the ground and all 28 states were marked out. A staff [member] then made this announcement, "We want you to ask God what state He would like you to intercede for. No Tamils praying for Tamil Nadu, no Nagas praying for Nagaland, no Maharashtrians praying for Maharashtra. Cross your borders." After some time, people began to stand at various places on the map.

"What the staff thought would be a 15-minute prayer session turned into a three-hour prayer session. Students asked forgiveness for their attitudes. Tears were shed as forgiveness was granted. Something had broken in the spiritual realm. From that day on, the students simply became Christians. There were no more Naga Christians, no Tamil Christians, no Punjabi Christians, they were just Christians."

*Editorial Note: I've known Sandra Liu for many years of my life. She is married to Ian Liu, and today they are both working in YWAM Chennai's Asha Kendra Christian School. As families, we've interacted many times. In my childhood years, Sandra was someone who treated me as a friend and not a child. She was also my teacher during my pre-teenage years. However, when I interviewed her, I saw a side of her I never knew. She described the person she used to be, and it was someone I never expected. I believe her story shows the transforming power of DTS.*

Her hands shook as she read the telegram which had arrived from home. Her father's health was failing and her family wanted her to return to Kolkata immediately. She had been in Chennai only for a week! Her mind raced in many different directions. Arriving here in Chennai to attend DTS had been a major decision for her, something she had been eagerly waiting for. But now this! She had only recently nursed her father out of a stroke. Once she was assured he was fully recovered, she had made preparations for DTS.

*Should I go home now and risk not being able to return for DTS? If I don't go and daddy dies, then I will be blamed.* As these thoughts tumbled over each other in her mind, she remembered a comment her aunt had made before she left. "You started college three months, and then you left. When they asked you to sing solo, you never went back because of fear. You never finish what you start." Sandra was a strong young woman with a need to prove herself to those around her. Back home in her neighborhood she was known as a "snob," a reputation she took delight in. She did not want to be known as a "quitter," and neither did she want to carry the blame if her father died. She felt responsible for her father's health, despite her mother and siblings being there.

When YWAM Chennai heard of her dilemma they rallied around her with prayer and support. She decided to remain in Chennai, waiting for a clear word from the Lord that she was to return home. None came. The days came closer to the start of her DTS. Despite feeling torn, Sandra desperately believed that her father was in God's Hands. Phone calls continued to come in for her, each one demanding to know what was keeping her in Chennai. The day before her DTS was scheduled to start, she received another phone call. She was tired of explaining herself, but anxious for any news about her father. This time the news was that her father was fine. Sandra could carry on with her DTS, something she had been looking forward to for a long time. One week's teaching in particular sticks out in her mind: Floyd McClung's "Roots and Fruits of Pride". *'Coming from a Chinese background there is a lot of pride, that we are the best, that we are self-sufficient, we won't ask for help, we won't be dependent on anyone. Even though India is my home, as Chinese we try to keep a step above everyone else.*

*We separated ourselves saying 'we are not like the Indians, we are not like everyone else',* Sandra reflected as she began to understand Floyd's message. To this day Floyd's words continue to serve as a guideline for her life.

DTS had now finished. The certificates were handed out and Tim Svoboda addressed the class. "Although your certificate means you've graduated, your real DTS is about to begin now. Once you return home, what you learned here will be tested by God." Sandra kept this truth close to her heart. At home, her sister Davina watched her like a hawk, scrutinizing her every action and response.

Things truly were different. Where she had once argued with her mother, she now responded lovingly. Sandra's mother still followed the Chinese ancestral worship. Red Chinese blessing papers hang along the walls of their home. On these papers, printed in gold are pictures of Chinese gods and demi-gods. Because she herself had been a Christian from an early age, Sandra never took part in this worship. But instead, she argued with her mother, trying in vain to turn her away from this worship. During DTS, Sandra learned she needed to give up her rights. Coming home Sandra's old behavior rose up to challenge her. She wanted to win the argument with her mother, she wanted to be right. However, she fought the temptation to voice her opinion, responding to her mother lovingly. She now knew she didn't need to raise her voice against everything she disagreed with. She let her mother worship. When her mother left the house, Sandra placed her hand on each of the blessing papers and rebuked the spirit behind them and continued to lovingly pray for her mother and the rest of her family.

The change in Sandra extended beyond her home life. In Kolkata she returned to her former teaching job. Before DTS, Sandra had often been the leader of any petition/protest raised by the teachers against the school's headmaster. After the students had left the classroom one day, Sandra was gathering her own belongings and prepared to leave for the day. The door opened, and one of her fellow teachers walked in with a paper in her hand. The paper was a petition. Many of the teachers had already signed it. She placed the petition on Sandra's desk, saying, "I know you have your own belief now so I will not force you to sign this. If you agree in your heart then sign this, but if you don't we won't force you."

More than passing YWAM's DTS, passing God's DTS had become of the utmost importance to her. Because of Sandra's dramatic turnaround, her sister Davina is involved in missions today. She told Sandra, "I watched you and saw that you had really changed. You were really mean before. I saw the change after you came back from DTS. I wanted the same thing you had."

*Editorial Note: Francis Balla attended DTS in Chennai in 1985 followed by a School of Evangelism (SOE). Francis' family have been Christians for four generations. Francis personally dedicated his life to the Lord in 1982, with the plan to go into missions. He thought that would mean preaching from a pulpit every Sunday. He never anticipated God would lead him into YWAM, with its living-by-faith lifestyle. But as he looks back on his years in YWAM, Francis doesn't regret a moment of it. In fact he commented that in the earlier days he thought, "If there is heaven on earth, YWAM must be it." Today, he is the City Coordinator of YWAM Hyderabad.*

Living by faith was an entirely new concept to Francis Balla. When he first heard about it in DTS, he was shocked. But he wanted to try it out for himself, to see if it really worked. One evening, a person approached him saying, "Francis, there is an envelope for you in the mailbox." Inside the envelope was 100 rupees and a note saying "Francis, we love you. Trust God for your finances." Francis held onto that command as he waited for God to prove himself.

God's "proof" came in an unexpected way. One day Francis was unusually hungry. He wasn't someone who usually ate in between meals, but on this particular day his stomach was making rumbling noises. He searched his pockets, but didn't have enough change to buy even a snack. The hunger grew stronger. Realizing this was a good opportunity to let God prove Himself, he prayed, "God, can you provide for me two *chapattis*?" hoping the ceiling would open up and deliver two *chapattis*. It didn't.

Francis' friend, Cassius Soares from Goa, came up to him. "Francis, I'm going to a restaurant, would you like to join me?" *What, you think I have a lot of money?* Francis retorted inside his mind. But he accepted the invitation. Cassius had made the invitation, he should pay. They sat down in a small restaurant not far from their house. Cassius ordered two *chapattis*[12] for himself and two for Francis. "This was exactly what I prayed for!" he thought. "Cassius could have ordered a *masala dosai*[13], something more common to Chennai. *Chappattis* aren't an ordinary meal item here."

"Cassius, I must tell you something," Francis said as he ate, now wishing he had ordered four *chapattis*. "I was hungry, and I asked God for two chapattis."

"You know, as I was about to leave the house, the Lord said to me, 'Francis is hungry, take him with you.'"

They both rejoiced. Cassius had heard and obeyed the voice of God, and Francis had learned living by faith actually worked.

*Editorial Note: When Jiggu Bogi joined YWAM Bangalore, living by faith was not a new concept for him. Before YWAM, he had been an assistant pastor at a church and before that had worked with Youth for Christ. As a pastor he received a minimal salary and often searched through his pockets for money to buy a meal. However, the greater issue Jiggu encountered was relating to foreigners, in particular British. This story is a particular time where he had to confront this very issue and how God dealt with him. It has a principle that speaks to all of us working cross-culturally or with the intent to in the future.*

"Hi," Jiggu smiled and waved as Matt walked toward him. Matt was from Britain and was serving in YWAM India at the time.

"Yes?" he said.

Jiggu smiled and waved again.

Again Matt responded, "Yes?"

Jiggu was furious. He couldn't return a simple hello. *These foreigners! They are all the same. They don't respect us. They think they are above us.* He had tried to be friendly and was met with rudeness.

As a child, Jiggu had listened keenly to each of his grandfather's stories of his life. Some of these stories included life under the British. One particular story involving the British he only heard once or twice, but as a little boy Jiggu took it to heart and became bitter toward the British. As both a village elder and a Christian, his grandfather garnered much respect from those living in his village. British missionaries also resided in the same village. There were occasions the missionaries asked his grandfather to perform menial tasks such as toilet cleaning, not realizing this was not expected of a man of his position. Jiggu's grandfather did it anyways, while the hurt built up inside his heart. When he heard this story, Jiggu picked up on this hurt and harbored bitterness toward the British, which also extended to other foreigners.

Later that day, there was a large meeting, where Matt was scheduled to speak. When he stood in front, he said, "I want to apologize on behalf of what the British did in India. I am asking for your forgiveness." Sitting in the back, Jiggu fumed. This same man, who had treated him so rudely, now had the audacity to stand in front and ask for forgiveness for the sins of the British.

Jiggu stood up, "I am not going to forgive you. You are worse than the British. They came in the name of their government and Queen, but you come in the name of Jesus and have the same attitude. I am not going to forgive you." Murmurs filled the hall. Nobody knew what to do. Sam Dharam walked to the front and said, "Let's forgive this brother. He has asked for our forgiveness. Come on, Jiggu."

"You forgive him, but I won't." Jiggu was adamant; there were too many stories in his past to give the man a clean slate in a second.

During the tea break, Jiggu sat by himself. Some Indians gave him a nod of approval as they went to have their tea. Thoughts were running through his head. A nagging thought kept cutting through his feeling that he was right in standing up to Matt. The nagging grew and became a conviction, and Jiggu knew what he had to do. But he still questioned. As he wrestled back and forth, he saw that what he was fighting against was not Matt's problem or the problem of the British, but it was his own internal problem. He let himself believe he was inferior to foreigners and because of that wasn't able to develop deep meaningful relationships with them. At the core of everything, it was this frustration that had caused him to yell out. He never had a problem relating cross-culturally but had no desire to develop deep relationships with any foreigners. He had to forgive and let go of the hurt from his past. He was just as valuable as any other British, American or Australian. Although the British had treated India wrongly, he needed to give Matt a chance.

He walked over slowly, worrying what he would say. Jiggu couldn't stop the tears as he said to Matt: "I'm sorry for the way I reacted. I'm sorry for blaming you for all the problems of the British and heaping my problem on your head. Please forgive me."

Matt accepted the apology and wrapped his arms around Jiggu. People around stopped their small-talk and turned their full attention to Matt and Jiggu. Some approached and laid their hands on the two of them, praying for both.

He let go of Matt, his face still wet with tears. Inside he felt a releasing sense of freedom. His own internal hurt dealt with, he saw a distinct change in his cross-cultural relationships. He was able to develop friendships at a deeper level and no longer had to carry his hurt with him. That day, Jiggu realized that cross-cultural relationships could never get below the surface if he had issues in his own heart that he hadn't dealt with yet. By releasing forgiveness and realizing his own worth, Jiggu was able to experience cross-cultural relationships in a new way. Since then, Jiggu has traveled and worked with an open heart alongside people from and in countries around the world such as the US, Canada, Scotland, Switzerland, Australia and many others.

**9**

# Trust God or Die

*ithin just two years of moving to India, my cultural world had expanded dramatically. Inside the YWAM community, my little ears were now accustomed to a variety of accents: the fast rolls of Tamil, the crisp British diction, the jovial Aussie accent, the rhythmic sounds of Samoan, the lilting tones of Chinese, the strong American accent and the musical pitch of Bengali. At celebrations, I had seen the Samoan slap dance performed, and glimpses of Bharatnatyam (a South Indian classical dance). My mouth had tasted foods ranging from bland jam sandwiches to fragrant, hot curries. This mixture of cultures had become "normal" to me.*

*Out of all these cultures, one that brought a particular vibrancy to our community was the Pacific Islands culture. Our islander friends came from places like Tonga, Samoa and Fiji, and their love of life and spontaneous fun charged the environment.*

*They were often the ones who initiated the laughter. They were also known for their willingness to sacrifice their own comfort and security for the sake of the Gospel.*

*One of the first Pacific Islanders to work with YWAM in South Asia was Leaula Aufai of Samoa. Leaula's calling to South Asia came while he still worked at his family's farm in Samoa. The hardships he faced and his own lack of knowledge regarding India's people, culture, and practices did not deter him from following God's call. And it was here in India that God summoned him to Bangladesh, a challenge he enthusiastically took.*

*The more I learned about Leaula's story, the more amazed I became at what has been accomplished through him in Bangladesh. Leaula followed his call to missions as my parents had – by doing a DTS – in Honolulu in 1983. He chose that location because of its focus on South Asia. He arrived from Samoa with US$3 in his pocket and his school fee of US$1800 not yet paid. Such was the start of Leaula learning about God's faithfulness with finances.*

*Following the DTS, he enrolled in the School of Evangelism. The school's outreach took him to Kolkata where he remained, assuming it was his mission field. There were many Bengalis [a major ethnic group in Bangladesh] from nearby Bangladesh in Kolkata, and soon God made it clear to Leaula that his call was not to India but to Bangladesh. Leaula moved there in 1985 when the country was still under military rule. Lessons learned in his years of working on the farm proved valuable to his success in Bangladesh. He knew well that it took a long time for seeds he planted to come to harvest, and that success required commitment and perseverance.*

*In 1990, he married Corina Alexander, the first Bangladeshi to do a DTS (in Uluberia). She had been working with YWAM in both India and Nepal since the early mid-80s. Corina's family provided Leaula with a place to stay when he initially came to Bangladesh. Today he lives in Dhaka with Corina and their two boys. Here is his account of that first year in Dhaka.*

# A Foothold in the Muslim World

"Leaula, you are the person to be going to Bangladesh, not me." Steve Cochrane placed his half-eaten club sandwich on his plate and wiped his mouth with the orange napkin.

I stared at Steve, shocked to hear him say this. Steve had always felt he was the one to pioneer YWAM Bangladesh, feeling called to the Muslim world. I had also felt a strong call toward the Muslim world and this small, river-laced country in particular. In the end, Steve trusted my conviction over his own. He never discouraged me from going, but I hadn't felt his complete blessing yet. It wasn't until our conversation in this airport restaurant that he finally accepted that his future was in India and mine in Bangladesh. Now he was releasing me, though I knew he was apprehensive about sending me there alone. With Steve's blessings, I could leave on that plane with no regrets.

"Steve, do you really mean that?" I asked.

"Yes, Leaula. I've spent much time in prayer. My place is here in India. You're the right person to begin YWAM in Bangladesh."

"That means so much to me. Thank you."

"But you won't be there without the prayers of your YWAM family. I'm sending you confident God will take care of you. But I still worry. I wish I could send you with a team and some money, but there is neither."

I nodded. Both fear and excitement rose up within me. The fear of the unknown and being alone simmered as I listened to Steve excitedly narrate to me his last trip to Bangladesh where he took an SOE team from Singapore at the beginning of 1984. Goosebumps prickled on my skin as I listened to Steve and imagined myself in that place in just a few hours. I wanted to board my plane now. My stomach growled so I made myself stay put, taking a bite of my sandwich. I was committing myself to Bangladesh for an indefinite amount of time with just US$30 to my name, unsure how I would provide for myself.

"We should get you on that plane." Steve said with a glance at his watch, "I'll come and visit you. But my work is here in Kolkata. Who knows how long I will be here?" We shared a laugh.

There were no YWAM connections in Bangladesh. However, the brother of one of our first Bangladeshi students, Corina Alexander, would meet me. I planned to live with his family for some time.

The guard glanced at my boarding pass. Everything was in order. With a bored flick of his hand, he motioned for the next person. I turned around for a final smile and waved at Steve.

"Please prepare for take-off," the pilot's voice came over the loudspeaker. As the plane lifted off, I took a last look at Kolkata. The Hooghly River looked like the trace of a finger drawn across a bustling city. When I first came to Kolkata, I proudly offered myself as a martyr, assuming this was where God had wanted me to live and die. However, by my sixth month, I heard God clearly calling me to Bangladesh. My heart was set upon Kolkata and West Bengal, and I didn't want to hear this. But knowing I needed to listen to His voice, I set aside time to fast and seek His confirmation. After three days of fasting, I was shown the role I was to play in the Muslim world, specifically in Bangladesh. God's question to me was, "It might cost your life. Are you willing to die in Bangladesh?" And I said yes.

The plane's rough landing in Dhaka, Bangladesh, awoke me to the reality that I would be walking out that promise to God from here on. The immigration official stamped my passport, and I walked out of the airport, laden with my guitar, suitcase and expectations. The streets were wider than what I had anticipated. Cycle-rickshaws abounded on the road, outnumbering motor vehicles. In terms of crowds, this wasn't much different than Kolkata; people still flooded the road, living and working on the streets. The buildings were more modern than what I had seen in India. I had expected Bangladesh to be less developed than India, but that was definitely wrong.

When I arrived, the country had only been independent for 14 years. After a power-share wrestle between East Pakistan and West Pakistan, ten million refugees fled to Kolkata, where they set up a provincial government. In late November 1971, they gathered the Indian army to their side and went to war against Pakistan. On

December16, 1971, Bangladesh became an independent nation.

Bangladesh is surrounded on its north, east and west boundaries by India. The Bay of Bengal rests at Bangladesh's southern border and Burma at its southeast. The numerous lakes which run through the country often flood each year. These devastating floods have been one of the factors hindering Bangladesh's economy and development.

The country's population is 86% Muslim and less than 1% Christian. I knew well what a huge task lie ahead of me. My goals for Bangladesh centered on church planting. To do this, networking with the other few Christians in Bangladesh was important. I needed their wisdom. But finding a trusting and eager person was nearly impossible. Out of all the Christians who surrounded me, there was just one who believed in me: the Assembly of God Church pastor. The church in Bangladesh dismissed me as young, naïve and inexperienced, waiting for the day I would leave the country in resignation. Missionaries I met always asked me three questions: *How old are you? Have you done Bible School or seminary? Do you have much financial support?* The answer to the first question was 22; far too young to their forty-something eyes. The answer to the last two questions was no. In the missionaries' eyes, those three answers disqualified me for the job.

Although this skepticism was difficult for me to digest, the missionary's doubts were reasonable. To them I was just another young missionary from a young organization, and probably not capable of completing my commitment. Also, the news of YWAM missionaries being arrested in Nepal on religious charges had reached here[14], and at present the name YWAM had a risky connotation. In light of this situation, the missionaries wanted to be sure I was sincere and well-equipped for this Bangladesh venture. I had quite a balancing act to walk in living out my call to this country. I had to still their doubts and redeem myself in their eyes, convincing them of God's call for me here. But in light of what they knew about YWAM, their doubts were not unreasonable.

I had never done Bible school (except for YWAM's DTS and SOE), but I didn't dare tell the missionaries I hadn't finished my last year of high school. I had very little financial support. When

my language and rent fees were paid, I had little money left. Often
it was just enough to buy flour, sugar, and tea leaves. I lived on
tea, *roti*[15], and flour balls that I made by mixing flour with boiled
water.

On one day, I had absolutely no food in the house, and only
70 *paise*[16], which even then, was not enough to buy a substantial
meal with. I searched under every cushion, in my drawers, inside
every pocket of my clothing, anywhere I could think of but could
not find any extra change. The Assembly of God Church was about
a kilometer and a half away and I walked there to see if any money
had come in for me. Nothing had come in, so I tried to figure out
what I could buy with my 70 *paise*, as I was really hungry now. The
long walk and the excessive heat and sun had only made my hunger
worse. There was a small restaurant and a grocery store, which
was owned by my friend, near to where I lived. First I went to the
grocery store and asked my friend how many *puris*[17] I could buy
with two *takas*[18], trying to calculate what 70 *paise* could buy. It was
too embarrassing to say I only had 70 *paise* left.

One *puri* would cost me 50 *paise*, leaving me with 20 *paise*. I
ignored the strange look I received at the restaurant when I asked
for one *puri*. Trying to hide my desire to stuff all of it in my mouth,
I took a small bite and smiled. I tried framing myself as a tourist
who was trying a *puri* for the first time.

Later a beggar asked me for money, I gave him 10 *paise* and
with my remaining money brought a *goja*[19], for an amount less
than what even a self-respecting beggar would buy.

The second day went by and still no money. The third day went
by and still nothing had come in. That evening a friend came by
with a surprise. She had received money and offered to take me out
to the only five-star hotel in Dhaka, the best restaurant in town.
I feasted that night on ribs and at the end of the meal my friend
presented me with US$86!

My stomach full, I went to the roof of where I was staying,
armed with my guitar like I did every evening when I was alone.
Tonight, I thanked God for His provision, but I also asked Him
why I had to go so long without food. Was there something He

wanted me to learn? His response was, "Son, it was not that I didn't want to provide for you, but I wanted you to learn how the poor of this nation live." I broke down in tears. It was only three days and nothing compared to what they went through week after week, but now I understood the pain, the search for money, the search for anything to fill the stomach. There was such a joy in my heart as I understood. Some of the future staff of YWAM Bangladesh were likely to be from this type of background, and I had to know how to effectively help them. A hope was planted inside me again; a hope that one day I would see Bengalis professing a faith in Jesus Christ, and that one day I would see them spreading the Gospel not only in their own country, but to the nations of the world. I knew the road ahead was going to be hard, but I was willing to die in order to see Bangladesh become a beacon of God's truth.

Every evening around six or seven, I was on this rooftop, with my guitar. It was here on the roof I was able to process my thoughts, my questions, my disappointments and my joys. Being by myself, the day's events and the missionaries' questions replayed themselves in my mind. The tears came easily. I felt alone, I felt as if no one cared what I did in Bangladesh. I poured out my frustrations to the Lord and returned to His promises to me. I had to inch forward one step at a time and believe something magnificent was waiting at the end. In Kolkata, we lived by the motto, "Trust God or die". It governed my life here.

With the guitar on my lap, I picked at the strings. The lights of Dhaka were coming on as darkness fell. A joy rose in my heart as I watched the lights. The lights for me came to represent the word of God, the hope that one day Bangladesh would be a nation shining forth the truth of God's light. On the rooftop I worshiped, claiming God as the one true God, claiming Bangladesh as His. My theme song I clung to that year was, "He is the living God enduring forever and His Kingdom shall not be destroyed." I cried out to God for the Bengali people and returned constantly to His Word, trusting His faithfulness to His promises. If it wasn't for this, the discouragement that came at me every day would have torn me apart piece by piece. It was from the small things I gathered my courage.

These small things were in the schedule I made for myself. I visited three different areas a week, praying as I walked around these areas, declaring them for Jesus, and sharing the Gospel with interested Bengalis. Generally, I found that people were not receptive to hear the Gospel. Prayer-walks were something I did a lot, as a result.

One of the places I visited every week was located on the other side of Dhaka and across the river. To get there I would take a 30 minute bus ride and then hire a boat to take me across. One particular week I had no money for either the bus or the boat, so I decided to ride my bike to the riverbanks and then swim across. But when I woke up that morning, my bike had a flat tire, and my only other option was to walk. My shoes were falling apart and would not last the couple hours of walking to the river. I instinctively knew the enemy was trying to defeat me and I determined not to let him win. I would walk there regardless. Before I left there was a knock on my door. A friend had arrived with five takas, it was just enough to pay my bus fare and the boat across the river and back. That river is known as one of the dirtiest in Dhaka, and I was not looking forward to swimming in it.

On Sundays, I attended an Assembly of God church. I met Mr. Haque here, a Bengali Muslim convert. He had met Steve on his previous trip to Bangladesh. We quickly struck up a close relationship, largely due to this mutual friendship. We spent hours in the back of a cycle rickshaw. As we bumped along, Mr. Haque pointed out buildings, places of interest, explaining the city of Dhaka to me.

Mr. Haque and I spent our Saturdays in the market, passing out tracts and sharing the Gospel with those interested. We found few receptive hands, and even fewer receptive hearts. A tract was rejected with a spit, and sometimes curse words. But we continued.

On a particular Thursday during the month of Ramadan, we sat with the brick breakers. They broke bricks 20-25 meters from the mosque. The bricks are broken into smaller pieces and mixed in with the cement to strengthen it. This is a main source of income for many in Bangladesh and often whole families are employed.

For the past few weeks we had been reading the *Injil* (New Testament)[20] to them as they were illiterate. People on their way to the mosque had begun to notice, and we sensed they were annoyed about these readings. A few weeks after we had begun reading the *Injil* to the brick breakers, I looked up to see an approaching mob. I froze. Out of the corner of my eye I saw Mr. Haque sitting very still as well. The *Injil* just lay in my lap. In front of us now, one person emerged from the mob and said, "What do you think you are doing?"

I stood up and explained I was reading the *Injil,* to these people who were interested. Mr. Haque was translating for me. The mob had one agenda; to beat Mr. Haque and me up. They were especially upset that I, as a foreigner, was there. No amount of explaining would calm them down. But as I tried to reason with them, I was fervently praying they would calm down and spare us.

But the mob only became more unruly, and I began to fear what might happen next. I felt a hand enclose around my own and pull me away from the crowd. I turned to see who it was. A small white cap was perched on his head. He was a Muslim. Fierceness glowed in his eyes, as he beckoned me to follow. The crowd was noisy, just a cacophony of sounds. He pulled me away from the crowd. Mr. Haque followed behind us.

"Look, you need to leave now," the man said. "Get out now! They will beat you up if you don't leave now." He gave me a small push. Mr. Haque and I started to walk away. I glanced behind me quickly. A fist rose above the crowd. The cheers of the crowd were led by one loud voice. My heart raced. We had to get away quickly. I did not want to be in the middle of a crowd whose only goal was to beat us up. The man who pulled us away from the crowd was our angel that afternoon. He was a Muslim; he could have joined the men and beaten us. But something prodded him to caution us.

That was the closest time I ever came to danger. Nevertheless, Mr. Haque and I continued to pass out tracts and share the Gospel. We pressed on, despite the discouragement that persisted to nag us. At the end of my first year in Dhaka, I returned to Honolulu to staff an SOE for three months, with the hopes of recruiting more workers. One of the outreach teams was headed for Bangladesh, and

I was leading that team. Four people stayed on after their outreach. I finally had partners!

Looking back now, I am thankful that Steve Cochrane released me to go to Bangladesh. Although that first year was filled with many hard lessons and trials, I can honestly say it was one of the best years of my life. I learned what it really means to trust in God. I was very inexperienced, but I let nothing stop me from what I knew God was calling me to. I had always loved challenges and still do today. But that first year in Bangladesh was no doubt one of my biggest challenges. God faithfully remained by my side and still does today here in Bangladesh more than two decades later!

*Editor's note: From the time of the first DTS in Dhaka in 1990, YWAM Bangladesh has grown to 100 staff with bases in five major cities. Presently, Leaula is the Regional Director, as well as responsible for Frontier Missions and the Neighbors Ministry.*

# 10

# Woman on a Mission

Since its beginning days in South Asia, YWAM has placed women in leadership roles and other positions of influence. They have taught in schools, counseled students, and led ministries. This practice sometimes has shocked nationals and people from other Christian ministries. But YWAM leaders persisted because of their belief in this as a biblical value.

Throughout my years in India I have seen many changes in attitudes toward women. I remember as a young child pointing out the rare sight of a woman driving a moped. Now female drivers have become commonplace. Women once had opportunity for only one kind of office job — that of a secretary. Today many women hold various full-time jobs in offices, from the administrator of a department to the CEO of high-profile companies.

These changes are most visible in urban areas. Outside, in the villages and rural areas, men fiercely hold onto their traditional belief that a woman's rightful place is in the home. I have observed that many of these women keep silent with their eyes downcast when in the presence of men. Their traditional role is to produce (male) children, to learn and perform the proper duties of the household; and to submit to their husbands in virtually all family decisions. Many women have accepted this position as their fate, and if they sense any inferiority they usually don't feel the freedom to express it.

Because my environment was mainly YWAM, these social rules were not in my community. There I felt valued on the basis of my personality and not my gender. But when interacting with the wider community, I felt restricted because of what others believed was my role as a female. Although some areas have changed for women, some things remain the same. It is easier to change external appearances than it is to change the behavior of the mind.

The Bible does speaks clearly of a woman's equal value with men. Jesus treated women with respect and kindness. He did not draw a dividing line between them and place one on a higher level. YWAM has approached the issue of women in authority in much the same way. Their process of decision-making relies on the person's qualification and not their gender. Because of this, the core beliefs of some were shaken. Other women felt affirmed and that they had found a place to belong. Steve Cochrane stated this about men and women's role in YWAM, "God is going to call certain male leaders to be Mordecais, to release the Esthers." Many of the men in YWAM have taken on this role, opening doors for their sisters and continually encouraging them to live fulfilling and successful lives.

Anima Martin is one who has felt this blessing and support from male leaders in YWAM to step into the fullness of her calling. Because of her struggle with Indian traditional attitudes toward women, Anima has a burden to reach out to women hindered by these beliefs and to help them to reach their goals. When I talked to her, she said the best way to empower women is to change society's attitudes and beliefs about them. I believe her strategy addresses the root of the problem. A woman can believe anything is possible for herself, but she may never achieve her dreams if her path is *obstructed by people who believe that a woman's only place is in the home.*

*From a young age, Anima Martin had big dreams. She was inspired by the stories of Mother Teresa and Pandita Ramabai[21], and she wanted to follow in their footsteps of serving God. When preachers and teachers visited her village, she admired them, hoping one day to have a life similar to theirs. At the age of 11, Anima gave her heart to the Lord. Since then, she has felt a specific call to minister to women. When searching for a life-mate, one of the characteristics Anima wanted was someone who would release her to live out the full potential of her giftings and callings. She found this in Simon Martin, who has backed her 100% in her ministry. Simon and Anima are the parents of three boys whom she is home schooling today in Pune. Despite the heavy workload of teaching, Anima has big plans to conduct seminars, to do TV shows and to write articles —all geared toward empowering and influencing the upper middle-class women of India with Godly principles. Here is Anima's story of how she started on this journey.*

# Raising Up Women of Faith

When I was four years old, my parents followed the call of God to Aalthaguri, a village in the northeast Indian state of Assam. My father was a pastor, and he went there to begin a new church. It proved to be a challenging assignment. At that time, Aalthaguri consisted of 10-15 mud huts, and its residents were uneducated and very poor. They depended on agriculture for their living, but most were neglecting their fields. It seemed that the whole village had lost any motivation for working. The children of the village did not attend school, and the adults turned to liquor to lighten their dismal mood.

Despite this heaviness of spirit, I found the village to be a beautiful little place. Located on a fertile plain just 16 kilometers from the border of Bhutan, Aalthaguri enjoys seasons of summer, monsoon, and spring. A short walk away was a town where we could buy supplies and a river where many of us children spent our time playing.

Besides giving the usual services of a pastor, my father helped the villagers in other ways. He showed the people how to cultivate their land properly, and soon they were growing and selling their own vegetables. He encouraged parents to send their children to school and stressed the value of education. As the villagers became self-sufficient, a new sense of hope for the future was born.

The mindset of my village regarding women was typical of Indian rural society. It wasn't until I moved out that I saw the effect it had on me. One day, when I was 10 years old, I was sitting with my legs propped up. When my mother saw me, she immediately reprimanded me for unladylike behavior. "Drop your legs! Women do not sit like that," she declared. That was just one "don't" on my list of "do's" and "don'ts" for women I constantly heard.

I began to see clearly that females were suppressed, and it upset me and raised a lot of questions in my mind. I wanted to know why women had to behave a certain way, while men could do whatever they liked. I wanted to know why men got the finest selection of the fish while we women got the remains. I wanted to know why women weren't allowed to do certain jobs. When I sought answers to my questions, the reply I received was, "This is how God has created women." The message I received was that women don't have much value.

This became more evident as I grew up and observed my friends becoming involved in relationships with the boys in our village. When a problem occurred, the girl was always blamed. If the two became involved in immoral behavior, people inevitably would say the girl enticed the boy into the relationship. The boy always walked away innocent while the girl had to suffer the consequences of her actions, even if both were at fault. Never once did I see blame placed on the boy for immoral behavior. One of my friends liked a particular boy. When they were seen talking, gossip about the relationship got back to the boy's parents. They disliked my friend and banned her from seeing their son. Like so many others I had seen, she was blamed for the initiation and continuation of the relationship.

There was another time when a woman returned to our village after completing her Bible school. She was asked to preach in the Sunday service, but many in the village voiced their disapproval. They said it wasn't her place to stand behind a pulpit and preach. As a woman, her place was in the home.

It is not only the men who maintain this attitude, but the women as well. Because for so long, this has been their place, they believe in it wholeheartedly. They believe their role in the home is an unchanging one, and one they have no right to deviate from. There is no need for a girl to continue with her education until 12th standard, as she will only remain in the home. When a girl becomes an adult, she marries and moves in with her husband's family. She is submissive to her husband who usually allows her influence over house affairs and nothing beyond that. This behavior has been followed for many years and few protest it.

Even though many women in the village accepted this as their fate, somehow I deviated from this, desiring more out of my life. I decided there was no need for me to marry. I didn't need a man, I could do quite well without one. Men would only transfer the blame to me. Men got the best of the family's supply. Men could sit around the house all day doing nothing, while girls had to sweep the floors and cook food. I figured I would save myself from the hurt I knew would come from associating myself with any man.

When I was age 17, I went to a town called Despur to study for a nursing degree. I had wanted to go to Bible school, but my father insisted that I learn a skill which would guarantee me a job. After graduation I remained in Despur, where I picked up an issue of the *Light of Life* religious magazine. Inside I spotted an advertisement for a Discipleship Training School, the first advertisement ever put out by YWAM Chennai. I had been praying continually that God would bring me to a place where I could learn more about the Lord and develop my relationship with Him. I knew I could go to a Bible school, but I wasn't keen to go through another long period of training. When I read about DTS, I instinctively knew this was what I had been praying for.

I contacted Chennai and they wrote back suggesting I inquire of schools from the Uluberia base as it was closer to my home.

Uluberia accepted me into DTS, but I had a three-month wait until the school started, so I returned home. My parents worried for me when I informed them of my plans. YWAM was unknown to them, and they worried it might be somehow connected to the Children of God cult. I assured them it wasn't, but they were still afraid for me. After all, I would be leaving the state of Assam for the first time, and knew nobody in Kolkata or Uluberia. At least in Despur, my parents knew the pastor who watched out for me. This pastor had offered to pay for my airfare and host me prior to my departure for Kolkata. On the day I was to leave, my father came to Despur with the intent of forbidding me to go to DTS. The pastor assured my father I would be fine and reminded him that if I didn't go I would lose the money on both the airfare and the DTS fees.

On October 8, 1984, the DTS began in Uluberia, and I came willing to do whatever it took to have more of God in my life. During the fourth week of our DTS, Brad Carr was teaching about humility. In one session, he focused on openness and brokenness. He emphasized that as a community we needed to confess issues that had built a wall between our relationship with God. He said it would lead to new freedom in our personal lives as well as our relationships.  By doing this in the safety of the DTS, there would be mutual accountability as we would be trustees of each others' issues.

I listened as they shared from their hearts and sobbed in front of the class. Then they were prayed over, and there was a definite change to their countenance. As I watched these transformations, I knew I too needed to confess my hatred toward men. This bitterness was slowly eating away at me. I wanted to hold onto it as a defense, but when I weighed it against my desire to have a deeper intimacy with Jesus all my hesitations disappeared. I walked to the front of the class and started to share about how I had grown up feeling suppressed as a woman. I told how seeing women's subordination infuriated me. I told how men's freedom and lack of accountability had sparked hatred toward them. I said that as a youth I was scared to enter even into a friendship with boys, because it was likely to be taken as romantic. I didn't want to be falsely blamed for enticing a boy when my only intent was friendship. I now found it impossible to just have a normal friendship with any man. As I shared these things, tears flowed down my face. I looked at the men in the class, and sincerely asked for their forgiveness. Some seemed shocked at what I had to say. Steve Cochrane asked some of the men to come up front. Standing there, they surrounded me, said they forgave me and then prayed with me. Steve asked that they pay heed to what I had said and to treat me as a Christian sister.

That day I felt a release in my spirit. But the issue didn't just vanish. Every time I saw any form of inequality toward women, the same bitterness returned its clamp around my heart. Once again I had to release forgiveness toward men in general. It was only as the years went by that I was fully released from this death grip of bitterness. Today, I can honestly say I am completely released from this. I am even happily married with three sons of my own!

For me, coming to YWAM was like entering a fresh new world. Before I had always felt the pressure to perform in order to be loved. I felt I had to behave a certain way as a woman and even just as a human being in order to be accepted. This happened not only in my village, but when I went away to do my nursing training at the age of seventeen. But from the very first day I joined YWAM, I felt an unconditional acceptance. From the beginning days, I felt I didn't have to do anything. I didn't have to put any effort into being accepted. I just was.

For our DTS outreach, we went to Nepal. The Smiths and Elisabeth Baumann took us trekking through mountain villages in Nepal. Our team was the one picked up by authorities and arrested on charges of proselytizing. Even after being released on bail, I remained as we had to return to court every six weeks to sign the *tariq* (a paper verifying we had not yet left the country). I staffed the first DTS in Nepal and generally helped to pioneer YWAM there. During this time Georgina Bennett was serving there and she spoke out this prophecy over me: "God will use you among women. I see many women, and you are standing in front of them teaching them." When I heard those words, I felt special, as if God had personally picked me from amongst the crowd.

A few months later, I returned to Kolkata. At the time I joined YWAM, we were still very much in the pioneering stages and many people were praying for a long-term call from God. I prayed and felt God was calling me to be a teacher. When I shared this with Brad, he wasted no time in drafting a letter and sending it out to our few centers around the country, announcing my availability for schools, even though I hadn't taught in front of a classroom yet. My first invitation came from Chennai for their DTS.

In Chennai, I taught on the character of God. The first day I was so nervous I had diarrhea! But I managed to get through the lecture and was amazed at how God used me. People were touched by God's love; there were tears as people realized the incredible love God had for them.

In 1987 Wendy Mahbert asked me to take over the leadership of RUTH (Reaching Unreached Through Homes), a ministry to women who were in their houses all day because of children and household chores. The girls who have worked with the RUTH ministry over the years share a common characteristic. These girls displayed a strong integrity and a commitment to share their faith through their actions and day-to-day living. There are countless stories of the influence their lives have had on others. I have seen them wading through thigh-high water during the monsoons to deliver food to the pavement-dwellers. Day after day they go out calling on needy women and children. Our YWAMers from Uluberia were blessed many times by their tremendous gift of hospitality.

The history of RUTH's ministry is full of stories of young girls who have discovered the different life offered in Christ Jesus. Often these girls return to their Hindu homes and community, but the RUTH teams have always given support to each one of these girls. Through my own involvement and in talking to the many people who have been involved with RUTH at some point or the other, I have seen a strong line traced through all their memories of the tremendous gift this ministry played in the lives of many women.

Our RUTH team employed no complicated methodologies. We simply went out in groups of two. Sometimes we met women who were out shopping and talked to them right on the street. But usually we would knock on doors, and more often than not, we were invited in. We inquired after a woman's emotional, physical and spiritual well-being. Since we timed our visits for mid-day and during the afternoon, the women were free from any urgent household chores. Most children were still in school, and their husbands at work, and supper did not yet have to be prepared. In this more relaxed atmosphere, we were able to speak more freely and to touch many lives. Sometimes young girls from these Hindu families came to spend the weekends with us.

Although our main focus was women, often we ended up influencing whole families, as the women would share what we had imparted to them. One particular family has continued passing on what we shared with them. The wife, Eva, had three young boys at the time we first visited. She was depressed and sometimes would ask us not to visit because she was too tired. We committed to visiting her once a week as a way to coax her out of her depression. Sometimes we brought food for her, other times we would take the entire family out for a picnic. Eva recovered from her depression and today she and her husband, along with two of their sons, are involved in missions.

RUTH was one of the first YWAM ministries started in Kolkata. It emerged at a time when women were rarely seen outside of their homes. Open-air evangelistic meetings attracted a variety of men because they were the majority walking on the streets. Most women were at home, and the Good News needed to be shared with them as well. Responding to this need was the reason the RUTH ministry was formed. While it no longer runs today, it helped stake out YWAM's foundations in Kolkata.

As I look back at different incidences in my life, I can see how my childhood experiences as well as my involvement in the RUTH team led to the burden I carry in my heart today for the women of India. In 1990 I married Simon Martin, who shares my desire to see women and men released into their areas of gifting.

My beginning days in YWAM were surely the birthing of this desire. My leaders were so trusting in allowing a young woman to travel around the country teaching in different schools. Their boldness and the trust they placed in me has encouraged me to do the same with others. I've been able to disciple many young women, one of whom is involved in leading DTSes today; another is today working in China; another working amongst the Rajasthanis;

and another with the Buddhists. It is very encouraging to see the boldness planted in these girls and their enthusiastic answer to God's calling upon their lives.

Although I've been involved in various activities over the years, I still carry the desire to see women's status strengthened. Women with children are of special importance. Children form a special attachment to their mothers, and mothers have an incredible opportunity to "feed" their children godly principles. If I can reach these women and teach them godly principles, they will in turn pass this teaching onto their children, nurturing a godly generation.

In rural pockets of India, there persists a strong belief in the model of a meek, submissive woman. However, within the urbanized context, this has radically changed over the years. Yet, the belief still persists in subtle ways, inhibiting women from achieving their dreams. To empower these women, one route to change involves helping men understand the equality of women and showing them how they can be the "door-opener" for women.

When I came into YWAM, I was accepted and soon released into what my leaders saw as my gifting. When Simon and I did our Leadership Training School in Hawaii, one week was focused on women in leadership. Loren Cunningham, the founder of YWAM, did something special that week. He asked the men in the school to gather around the women and pray a prayer of releasing for God's call upon our lives. During that time, I once again felt YWAM was where I belonged, because it accepted and affirmed women in their calling.

I believe God has a plan for women. For some this may be within their homes. But this is not the call for all women. I do not feel my role is to encourage all women to step out of their homes. Rather, I feel my call is to encourage and release women into the full potential of what God created them to be.

# 11

## The Explosion

June 1988. YWAM India was nearly six years old, growing steadily and moving forward with the unsteadiness of a toddler's legs. Since I had spent five of my eight years in India, I felt like I was growing up with YWAM. We both were slowly finding our way in India. I had embraced India as my home and my identity was intertwined with it. But like YWAM, larger identity questions awaited me.

In its first six years, YWAM's young leadership didn't spend much time strategizing about the future. They lived mostly in a daily survival mode, trusting God to sustain and guide them. But in 1988, a new wave was rising that would sweep the mission into an era of unprecedented growth and change. As I think back over YWAM's history in India, one of the most significant catalysts to this growth spurt was the GO (Global Outreach) Fest held in Mumbai in 1988.

*YWAM International began hosting weeklong GO Fests around the world in the late 1980s as a way to mobilize churches for missions. Seeing YWAM's development in India, international leaders approached YWAM India about holding their own GO Fest. YWAM India jumped to the challenge, electing Sam Dharam to head up the operations.*

*Many throughout YWAM South Asia viewed Sam's large plans and methods with skepticism. They saw his organizational work as unnecessary because the end results looked unattainable. But as time inched closer to the projected date, they understood more clearly the possibilities and became the cheerleaders.*

*Elisabeth Baumann (Cochrane), who worked closely with Sam in organizing the event, said in a recent interview, "The GO Fest got us believing again. We saw that we [YWAM South Asia] could really do something significant."*

*The GO Fest brought the mission new respect from the church in India. It also prompted YWAM leaders to seriously evaluate their methods and to pick up new organizational tools to move them into the future. It was through Sam Dharam that God led this change. Sam has been a frequent visitor to our home, and he is known as one of those rare leaders who have both vision and a grasp of how to implement it.*

*Sam was a senior business executive when he committed his life to the Lord in 1977. As a new Christian he felt a strong call to missions. In 1983 he resigned from his job to follow that call. A few months later he enrolled in YWAM Singapore's DTS, and he has been in the mission ever since. In 1986, Sam moved to Hyderabad, India, to pioneer YWAM in that city. His influence soon reached far beyond Hyderabad, bringing new professionalism and emphasis on planning to the mission. That influence multiplied after he took over as National Director of YWAM India in 1996.*

*Sam is what I call a practical visionary. He imagines the future in "big picture" format and can create a detailed roadmap to reach this "big picture". This gift proved an invaluable asset in the GO Fest. I was in awe when I first stepped into the huge tent where the event was held. Even as a child, I sensed something big was about to happen for YWAM. I could not have imagined then just how significant it would be. Here in the words of Sam Dharam is the story of that great event and its implications for YWAM South Asia.*

---

# Preparing for an Explosion of Growth

I stood alone in the large tent, facing the empty stage. Dust swirled off the floor where the chairs had once stood. Across the back of the stage, a banner hung. Printed in large blue letters it said, "GO Fest." The last five days spent under this tent had been beyond anything we had expected. I thought of the thousands of people from Mumbai and other cities who had crowded under this tent. I thought of the inspiring worship time we had and the powerful messages from each of the speakers. Awe overwhelmed me and all I could say was, "Thank you, God. This only happened because of You." It was nothing short of a miracle.

For the previous five days, people from different walks of life had filled this tent. Late-comers had to stand. When the crowd estimates were made, mouths dropped, and eyes widened—1,500 in the daytime, 4,000 in the evenings. People returned day after day, hungry for more spiritual food. Leaders representing 58 denominations from all over India had gathered together, intermingling with each other in an amazing spirit of unity.

This five-day GO Fest was the beginning of a new chapter for YWAM South Asia, and I was thrilled to be a part of it. Only five years earlier, I was living a far different life. At that time I was employed as a project manager for a construction company. The job allowed me to live a comfortable life, and I no doubt would have been promoted had I stayed with the company. But after becoming a Christian, I felt a strong call to missions. God led me to Singapore in 1984, and I enrolled in their DTS. That school changed me, and I knew YWAM was where the Lord wanted me. I joined YWAM in India because I wanted to give back to the country which had invested much in me.

The longer I served with YWAM, the more its loose structure of accountability concerned me. Each base more or less functioned on its own, developing a separate blueprint. For six years they had operated the organization by trial and error.

Most of the YWAM India leaders had one common characteristic — they were visionaries. Put them together in a room, and everyone spoke enthusiastically about their visions and dreams for the nation. The volume in the room rose with their excitement, one vision starting after another had barely finished. After six years, they hadn't changed much from the zealous pioneers with unique, broad visions. Unfortunately, they lacked the ability to put those visions into action.

I worked closely with Tim Svoboda who brought me into meetings with the other leaders because he wanted my input. At first I felt insecure offering suggestions to foreigners, especially those in leadership above me. Even though they viewed me skeptically, I boldly told them their visions would simply remain visions without a plan of action. God could make things happen, but He desired them to have a role in the planning.

At first, the group rejected management as unbiblical. These leaders saw themselves as pioneers, not administrators. They always wanted to wait on God and hear what He had to say. There was nothing wrong with this, but I felt they were missing another vital point, that God is also a God of management. The skills of pioneering and vision were good, but an organization wouldn't move forward if there were no other skills to work with. Slowly, they saw this fact as truth, and we started to look at their visions and plot how to translate them into reality. In the midst of this "new" strategy, we still continued to seek God for His direction.

Around this time YWAM was holding successful GO Fests around the world. Steve Goode was the first regional director of YWAM South Asia (which at the time also included Southeast Asia). Steve and his wife Marie were based in YWAM Thailand. Often many of the YWAMers went to Thailand to renew their visas, and the Goodes' home was where they stayed. Beyond being regional directors, Steve and Marie were spiritual leaders for many in the region. The international leadership of YWAM asked Steve to challenge YWAM

India to hold a GO Fest. He brought this opportunity to us, and we accepted. Tim Svoboda suggested that I be the head of operations. Elisabeth Baumann would be the "face" of YWAM India to YWAM International.

For us, it was the perfect opportunity to put YWAM South Asia on the map. But we also wanted the GO Fest to mobilize the participants to tell others about Jesus. The church of India needed a boost and a contemporary expression of evangelism with a stronger awareness for missions that would go beyond the needs of their own church.

In 1987, I went to Mumbai twice to network with leaders and pastors in the city. Then in February, four months before the actual event, we rented a two-room flat, and converted it into our office. The team grew from four people to more than 30 at the end. Taking the principles of empowerment, teamwork, delegation, accountability, trust and affirmation from my old job, I introduced them here. Some people wondered what I was doing. While focusing on the details of the GO Fest, I was thinking ahead to the GO Fest's effect on YWAM's future.

Any businessman would have regarded our minimal budget for the event as impossible. With meager resources, we started out anyway. We knew somehow the money would arrive. Letters were banged out on the good old typewriter. Tucking the letters into envelopes we sent them through the post, hoping they would arrive at the right destination, in the right hands, and in reasonable time. To save money, we walked to meetings instead of riding in taxis. Phone calls were made from a public phone booth.

Offerings poured in from all over YWAM South Asia, and a small amount from YWAM International. The largest contribution came from the Catholic Charismatic renewal and prayer groups in Mumbai. With this, we could rent equipment and a venue.

On the first day of the GO Fest, my emotions ran on high as I watched people register, file into the tent, and then settle themselves down in the chairs. At break time, people fellowshipped across denominations and generations under the *shamiyana*[22]. All had gathered with one common interest—to know God. I watched from the back of the tent with tears in my eyes. My heart was full of amazement and gratitude to God for bringing these people together. There were Pentecostal pastors clothed in their whites, Catholic priests in their robes, and young people wearing Western jeans and t-shirts.

Speakers came from all over India as well as outside. The opening speaker was from Thailand. When he was done, there was a single thought on people's mind: the impact of the church on society. Many of them left wondering why they hadn't approached it from this angle before. We had other speakers who spoke to the Indian's hearts through their emotionally and intellectually charged messages. Each had a challenge, leaving the audience with something to ponder. At night, music concerts filled the air. Although Mumbai was India's trendsetter, it was still somewhat traditional in 1988. We brought in rock bands. The young people loved them. As the young people responded to the Christian message in a way they hadn't in the church, a new evangelism form was accepted by those from traditional backgrounds. The GO Fest embraced various methods, showing one method could not reach all people.

Mumbai was chosen as the venue for the conference because of its symbolic importance to India. One of India's five major cities, Mumbai is the commercial capital of India, and the home of Bollywood, India's film industry. Because of its social and financial prominence, Mumbai is a main gateway of India. We knew that holding the GO Fest in Mumbai would have a symbolic significance and bring YWAM further into the limelight.

None of us expected the impact of the GO Fest to be as powerful as it was. In those five days we won the backing and respect of the Christian community of India, something we had sought for a long time. This was the first time the various denominations of Mumbai had gathered under one tent. I remember some of Mumbai's prominent pastors approaching me, marveling at how these denominations had come together. People had not come with their own agendas. When they left, the Great Commission was burning in their hearts.

After the excitement, evaluation, and the planning, everyone wandered off. I stood alone. A young boy at my side broke into my thoughts, "Sir, can you please move? We need to take the tent down."

I picked up my briefcase and headed for the large gates. I glanced back for one last look, and shook one last hand on my way out with someone who wanted to express his gratitude.

Something had changed in all of us. The leaders' implicit trust in me was one of the main things that made this GO Fest work. In my spirit, I felt something was radically going to change and pave the way for great things in South Asia. I had completed my task and would leave for Hyderabad tomorrow. I walked through the gates and onto the busy streets of Mumbai.

Those of us who organized this conference came together for one last meeting. Steve Goode shared with us his heartfelt emotions for the events of the past week. He talked about the necessity for structure. It was easy to see we could not continue to operate the way we had. At this meeting we discussed and prayed about who should be the National Director. In 1989, Tim Svoboda took up this role.

The first step toward organizing YWAM was forming the National Council in 1989, which was made up of some of the base leaders of YWAM India. I was at this meeting to help them strategize about their plans. Forming a mission statement and thinking in terms of "nation" rather than "bases", was a new and difficult bridge, but a necessary one to cross. To get them started, I said, "We're here to brainstorm. You all have some incredible visions, and we need to move forward in a larger way than before. To start, how many workers do we want by 1993, in five years?"

After much time of waiting on the Lord and sharing our hearts Debbie Carr crystallized our thoughts and said, "How about 1,000?"

I stood up slowly and walked to the blackboard and wrote down the figures people proposed. One thousand workers by 1993. YWAM centers in 22 cities. Ten DTSes. Turning to face them, I said, "All right, if we want 1,000 workers in five years, how are we going to get there? How many DTSes are we running right now a year?"

"One in Kolkata," said Steve.

"Two a year, sometimes three in Chennai," Tim offered.

"And one here in Mumbai," I said.

"Don't forget they are also starting in Delhi and Hyderabad." Brad Carr suggested.

I wrote this information on the board. "Okay, that is about five a year." Doing some quick calculations in my head, I said, "If we don't increase the number, we won't have 1,000 workers until 2020. Our retention rate isn't too high."

There was a silence around the room as everyone took in these figures. Many had already thought we were at our highest performance rate, but it was news now that we weren't. Someone spoke up, "Okay, Sam how do you suggest we reach this goal?"

During the GO Fest, they had watched me carefully, viewing my approach with skepticism. Now I reminded them how my strategy translated a vision into action, making us a team. Management and spirituality didn't mix in their minds. They grasped a small part of the point I attempted to make, but were still hesitant about management, holding on to the faith that had brought them this far.

Before giving them the plan, I asked them to look at Daniel 6:1-2, to show them faith was inseparable from management. Here in the Bible, Daniel, a man of God was placed over King Darius' kingdom, over the administrators. King Darius was gifted with tremendous management skills and utilized a flow chart in his governance. Daniel played a valued role in the King's government. Those who objected to him could find no grounds on which to take him out of his role, except to make their own rules, which he surely would not follow. I used this passage of Scripture to show how God placed Daniel in a leadership position. God gifted a man with management to advance the Heavenly Kingdom. We could no longer look down on it as a lack of spirituality, it was now seen as a matter of spiritual integrity and responsibility. This one day we spent in the room, dreaming and planning, finally converted all of them. They had heard me say this before. But today they understood with their hearts. We sensed the urgent need for structure, management and planning. Many meetings followed where we plotted out the road ahead of us.

Here were men and women of vision, and now these visions were finally becoming a reality. It was an exciting time. To step forward, we needed more workers and visibility. We opened our doors wider for others to join us from around the world.

Within India, we started something called the 100-city project. The project's focus was to advertise YWAM in 100 cities all over India and show how it could serve the church. It was also aimed at recruiting more workers. My role was to standardize our methods, so that as our workers spread across India, they would communicate the same. This way there would be one clear message of who YWAM India was. Teams of two were sent into the nation, each team visiting a few of the 100 cities. Within six months, we reached all the targeted 100 cities. The teams returned with exciting reports of open doors across the country and the support of many local pastors.

This 100-city project made YWAM a visible organization in the country. Pastors and their churches understood who we were and expressed a desire to work alongside us. We had changed in a positive way but had not lost our essential core. Vision was still an important part of YWAM, but now management guided us. We became a real organization, rather than separate bases scattered around South Asia. We still dreamed our big dreams, but now we also had the tools to see those dreams become reality. We were no longer a group of excited, young naïve missionaries. Our ambitious visions and strong faith remained an integral part of us, but now we had gained the structure to put these into action.

# 12

# We Must Tell Them

*I first met Peter and Sharon Grant in October 2003. Just one question from me, and Peter was spilling out entrancing stories of their work in Nepal. I sat amazed at what this intrepid British couple had seen and experienced. Peter and Sharon Grant are fearless, passionate people. They have gone places under conditions that would stop most people cold. Sharon talks of trekking for several days while six months pregnant, as if it were a completely normal thing to do. They carried their one-year-old son on another mountain trek, and the only hint of complication they mentioned was melting ice into water to give him a bath!*

*I was deeply touched by their passion for the unreached. In the areas where they serve, a vast number of people have not yet heard the name of Jesus. Few are willing to travel to the hard-to-reach areas that are the least evangelized. But Peter and Sharon Grant seem to relish such a challenge.*

*Peter and Sharon both did their DTS in Singapore in 1989 after which they attended the School of Frontier Missions in Mussorie, India. Since then, they have spent years trekking through Nepal to bring the Gospel to various Himalayan peoples. They also are involved in teaching others what they themselves have learned about serving Jesus among the Tibetan and Nepali people. Today, these YWAM adventurers live in Kalimpong, India, with their five children. After talking to Peter and Sharon, I was filled with a longing to see more people like them venture out into unknown territory with a passion to see the Gospel penetrate every square centimeter of the globe. This inspiring couple have far too many stories to tell in this book, but here are two of their stories that I most enjoy. The first is narrated by Sharon and the second by Peter.*

---

# Why Has It Taken You
# So Long Too Come?

We had completed four months of language study in Tibetan and were ready to venture out. We chose the holiday time of Diwali (festival of lights) to trek to a remote valley north of Kathmandu. Before ascending the 5,000meter (15,000feet) pass, we rested at a small Sherpa house. Over a meal of flat bread and tea, the *Sherpas*[23] told us it would take two days to get over the pass, and there was no place to rest in between. As I heard these words, pain gripped my stomach and a great fear loomed up in me. At the time I was six months pregnant, and I think my maternal instincts were stirred up to protect our baby. But Peter and I felt as long as we could still walk and carry our bags we should carry on. After a few moments of prayer, the fear and pain left. Unfortunately, the bad weather outside had not left. The Sherpa village was being hammered by sleet and rain, and it was snowing up on the pass. Visibility was poor, and we knew it would be foolish to try to leave. We remained at the foot of the pass (4,000meter/13,000feet elevation) for a few days until the bad weather broke. Then we set out on our way, stocked with 14 pieces of flat Tibetan bread in our rucksacks.

To reach the top of the 5,000m pass, we first had to descend about 4,300m. The descent was so steep it made walking impossible. Our 30kg rucksacks pushed us into a Sherpa run. This is a term used to describe trekkers being propelled into a run down a hill by the heavy loads on their backs. A slippery rocky path was cut into the face of the cliff we were descending. Peter remained in front, continually looking behind to make sure I was okay. On one of those times, his rucksack caught on a rock outcropping. The weight of the pack pushed him forward. There was nothing I could do but watch in horror as he lurched toward his possible death. Then somehow his body miraculously sprang back to the wall. It was if an angel had him in his arms and pushed him back into the wall! It all happened so fast. We praised God that his life was saved. We carried on upwards and made it over the pass in just one day after the final 2,100m descent!

As we arrived at the village, we could see the men guiding the yaks into higher pasture. A young man approached us and remained by our side constantly, following us everywhere. We were careful about what we shared with him, as we suspected he might be a secret police. At the time it was illegal for Nepalis to convert to Christianity, and this young man could be looking for a way to accuse us. Our fears were first raised when Peter opened his guidebook, and the young man asked if it was a Bible. After spending every moment with us, even sleeping outside our window that night, he took us to meet his cousin, Mingma, who in turn told us the story of his brother, Galsang.

At the age of 12, Galsang was evicted from his village because of the spirits that possessed him. The villagers were scared of Galsang and didn't know how to control him. He was forced to live in an outlying jungle where his parents brought him food everyday. Year after year, his condition remained the same. Then one day a mysterious visitor appeared in the village. This 16-year-old boy looked vaguely familiar. The story he told amazed the villagers. He said, "Last night a person named Jesus came to me in a vision. He was full of light. When He came all the demons that possessed me left. The demons said 'someone greater than us has come, we have to leave you alone now.'"

The boy telling the story was Galsang. Through him this village heard about Jesus for the first time. This young man we had been afraid of was just one of the many villagers eager to know about this Jesus with power greater than the demons. It had been four years since Galsang returned, and the villagers were thirsty to know more about this Jesus. Because we were foreigners, Mingma assumed we were Christians and looked to us to explain who this Jesus was. We gladly went to his family and talked to them. They all accepted Christ.

Mingma, however still had questions for us. He said, "Why has it taken you so long to come here and tell us about Jesus? If this God is really true, and people out there know about Jesus, why don't they come and tell us? Why has it taken you so long to come here?" Peter and I were heartbroken by this question. We had no good answer to give Mingma. But we returned every month after that to disciple him and his people. The area this tribe – the Helmut Shepar – live in, is 100% Buddhist. To be a Christian here is like walking upstream in a swift Himalayan river. On Christmas day in 1991, we were able to have our first meeting resembling a church service.

Mingma's question to us that day became the motto by which we guided our lives. We simply could not wait for someone else to share the Gospel. We had to be the ones to answer the need. For if we didn't, then who would? The way we saw it was if everyone sat around waiting for someone else to do something, then no one would ever do anything.

Peter and I continued to visit new places and share the Gospel. We weren't readily accepted everywhere, but there was such a burden on our hearts we kept moving on. Mingma's words reminded us that many others were eager to hear what we had to share. Two years after we had been in Nepal, we revisited a place. When we had been here the previous time in 1990, I received a word from the Lord saying that this particular area would be a place of permanent light and witness. There was such a sense of excitement. We returned two years later to see the fulfillment of this word. I will let Peter narrate this, as the story involves an incredible revelation God gave him.

# The Power and the Glory

After five weeks and 240 km of walking through jungles and green paddy fields, my wife and I – along with our one-year-old son Joshua — reached a barren, cold desert at 4,000m elevation in a district called Mustang. We were returning to this area of northern Nepal in February 1992 in fulfillment of a word Sharon had received.

Apricot gardens and stone huts provided some color variation in the otherwise snow-covered landscape. When we reached the village, we began asking people if there were any Christians in the village. Each person we asked said no. Disappointed, we pressed on to the next village.

The mountain edged one side of the trail, and it was a sheer drop to the bottom on the other side. There was no guardrail to stop us from falling if we slipped. Snow and ice covered the path. As we continued to walk, I saw a small pathway veering to the right. Looking at my guidebook, I saw it wasn't even indicated or marked. But I felt an urge to take the path. When I looked up, Sharon was already walking up the path cautiously. With not a word to each other, I followed behind her. Joshua was peacefully sleeping in the carrier. The ice was thick in places and a strong wind threatened to knock us over. The snow whipped off the ground and blew into our faces. After walking three miles, we came upon a small village surrounded by a stone wall. Above the wall a row of white prayer flags were fluttering in the bitter wind. Knowing we had been led here, I jumped over the wall and waited for Sharon to pass Joshua over. A man was running toward us.

Without a greeting he immediately said, "You're Christians, aren't you?"

We remained silent under his assuming glare. The man's demeanor didn't welcome a positive response to this question. He carried on, assuming we were Christians, "You're not good. You've come to deceive us. Why have you come to this village?"

I ignored his assumptions. "We want to see how you live up in these mountains, what your culture is like. Is it okay for us to stay with you?"

The man stared for a few seconds. Then the hardened and offensive look on the man's face disappeared. Crinkles formed around his eyes and he smiled. He started quickly walking ahead, motioning for us to follow. His house was the first we came to in the village. People had braved the cold to come see who these newcomers were. The man opened the door saying, "Come in, come into my house."

Inside, we met the rest of the family members. Warm cups of tea were pressed into our cold hands, as they eagerly welcomed us. For some time, we all remained inside, answering and asking questions about each other. Soon, Joshua was passed from lap to lap, being entertained by each member of the family. While Sharon stayed inside with the man's wife and children, I spent the rest of the day helping the man prune his apricot trees in the snow and ice.

When nightfall came, Sharon and I settled down on our mat. Our bodies were exhausted, and we slept immediately. Early the next morning there was a knock. We quickly dressed, and I answered the door. It was the man who had welcomed us into his house.

"Had a nice sleep?" he asked.

"Yes. Thank you very much for letting us stay here."

"My pleasure," the old man grinned. With an earnest seriousness in his eyes he said, "Tell me, tell me everything you know about this Jesus of yours."

This man really believed we were Christians, even though we had never stated it. Here was a chance to share our testimonies. We invited him to sit down. As he shared, I felt God revealing the bondages of the trials he went through in following his own religion. Without addressing this directly, I was able to reveal a way out of his struggles to the man. The man's eyes and heart opened more with each word. I talked of Jesus' suffering, about the cross and the sufferings of the early church. After a few hours of talking the man stood up, his face alight. With conviction he declared, "I believe. This Jesus of yours is wonderful, He too suffered like us, He is now my Jesus." From the expression on his face, it was clear he had already accepted Jesus as His Saviour in his heart. He gently took both of my hands in his and exclaimed, "This is such good news, thank you, thank you!"

I was fearful he would not be strong enough. I was fearful of the consequences of his belief and wanted him to fully understand the decision he was making. So I said to him, "No, no don't believe. You don't know how much trouble this could cause you."

But his face only shined more. He was excited.

I gave him a challenge, "If this is such good news, then is it good news for the rest of the village?"

The man's eyes widened. He released my hands and ran out of the room. My wife and I looked at each other, puzzled. A few minutes later, he reappeared at our door again, telling us to come to the front room. Many of the villagers were there seated, anticipated looks on their faces. We shared our testimonies with them. That day, many of them dedicated their lives to the Lord. But I wanted to show them something more; I wanted to show them the power and reality of Jesus.

We moved the meeting onto the man's flat roof, hoping that up here people would be able to witness God's power if He chose to show it. The air was still. The snow from the blizzard of the previous day was still on the ground, but there were no whistling winds and blinding flurries. The sun had broken through the clouds and provided some warmth to fight off the stinging cold. In that remote mountain village, I talked about God's power and His promise of never leaving us. As I finished talking, I noticed down below that a bent and weathered old man was shuffling slowly past us.

"Are you sick?" I shouted down to him.

"Yes," he croaked back.

"Do you want to get healed?"

"Yes." I motioned for him to join us on the roof. His shoulders hunched, he walked over slowly, taking short, quick gasps of air.

When he was standing beside me, I faced the new believers.

"This is how we heal the sick. First we talk to Jesus and ask him what we should say or do." I bowed my head. God spoke to me about this man's lifestyle. The man smoked heavily and was inflicted with tuberculosis. I shared with the man the revelation I had received.

He collapsed to the ground. His shoulders shook violently. I bent down to lift his face and saw tears streaming down his wrinkled face. He said he wanted to be healed, but not only that but he also wanted to serve Jesus. Right then, both of those requests were granted. I prayed what happened today would live on as an example after I was gone, and the new believers would refer to this day as the proof of God as an absolute power and one they could call on for healing. I wanted them to witness God's power themselves and believe. I did not want them to blindly believe in my words, not really understanding the depth of this concept. God had granted them that very opportunity, and He had also transformed the life of this man.

Later on in the day, when people had gone back to their houses, talking in excitement about what had just happened, I quietly slipped off to a place outside the village. Finding a somewhat dry stone peeping up from the snow, I sat down. I praised God for what had happened today, for the miracle of the entire village accepting Him. Then God said to me, "What day is it today?"

"Well, Lord you know more than me what happened today, it's awesome, it's remote, miles away from any church, and these people are coming to your Kingdom." But God repeated the question, "What's so special about today?"

I thought about it, not too sure what He was referring to if it wasn't the new believers. When I thought about the date, that's when I realized. It was February 12, 1992. Four years ago, I was on the British cross-country skiing team for the Olympics Biathlon. Before leaving for this trip I received a letter in Kathmandu from the British Olympic Committee. They were inviting me to represent them at the 1992 Olympic Games. Today was the day I should have been there. I could be cross-country skiing, competing against the world, competing for a gold medal to honor Britain. But here I was in this isolated place, sharing the Gospel with people who had never heard it before. I wasn't even going to attempt weighing the difference of the two events. God has quite a sense of humor and an incredible plan far beyond what I could have imagined.

Surrounded by the immense mountains of the Himalayas, I had my own Award Ceremony with God. I had given up my chance at the gold for something greater. In recognition of what was meant to happen and what actually did happen that day, the Lord said, "These are your medals." These medals mattered more than any Olympic medals, because these medals honored something greater than country. These medals honored God.

# Waves of the
# Second Generation

*O*ne major goal of YWAM South Asia's pioneers has been fulfilled. Today most of the mission's workers and leaders in the region are nationals. Although some of the foreign pioneers continue to work in South Asia, they are content to remain in the background so that nationals can continue to be released. While YWAM South Asia's work is progressively indigenizing, it retains YWAM's trademark diversity. This diversity is defined by both the cultural and religious backgrounds of its workers.

Two decades of YWAM in South Asia have passed, and we now see a second generation stepping up. I use the term "second generation" not in its traditional sense, but to recognize new leadership stepping forward. Some of these leaders have been working in YWAM for years and are just now rising up. Others have recently joined YWAM, and are faithfully carrying on the vision given to them by earlier leaders. This second generation is bold, sharp, and visionary. They have the backing of leaders who have *done (and will do) all that is necessary to see them released into their full potential. This second generation represents the citizens of India, Nepal, Bangladesh and Sri Lanka. They are the ones now holding the torch and sprinting with it. They are going places and reaching people groups that aren't easily accessible. It thrills my heart, and I know it thrills the hearts of many others, to see this movement happening.*

*Here are the stories of a few of these hard-working individuals. Although these stories focus on Indian leaders, they represent the heart and vision of other South Asian nationals.*

---

# Baskar - An Angel of Mercy for Street Children

After watching the skit for the third time, 21-year-old Baskar knew what was coming next. A man in a long black coat walked across the grass, laughing wickedly, as he cracked his whip of bright-colored sections. He circled a man squatted on the grass who held his head in his hands. Baskar watched, identifying with the man on the grass. Baskar's search for happiness on the streets of Hyderabad had failed. He felt lonely and fearful and hopeless.

A man dressed in a white robe walked across the grass, and pushed the man in black to the ground. He lifted the crouched man to his feet and wrapped his arms about him. Something he said to that man brightened his face, and he was no longer sad and afraid. Baskar wondered who the man was and if the same could be done for him.

After the actors began to pack up, Baskar approached the man in white to ask if he could help him become happy. The answer was yes, and Baskar heard about Jesus for the first time. He had never believed in any god before, but this day he made a decision to believe in this Jesus and make Him his Savior. The man in white called two other actors, and the three of them prayed with Baskar. A burden lifted off of his heart. It was simple, but so wonderful! An address was given to him scribbled on a small slip of paper. He went soon, eager to have help in his new faith. The address sent him to YWAM Hyderabad in Shanthi Nagar.

Seven years earlier, at the age of 14, Baskar had run away from home. He was lured to Hyderabad by the prospect of a glamorous city job. The lures were just a mirage. The only job he was able to get was as a tea-server in a restaurant. Each night, he walked to the train station, and laid down on the platform to sleep, despite the traffic of people and trains. Feelings of emptiness and rejection covered him like a heavy blanket.

Arriving at the YWAM centre, Sam Dharam, the director, warmly greeted Baskar. Even though it was his first meeting, Baskar felt comfortable here and shared with Sam about his life on the streets. Baskar kept his contact with Sam and other YWAM Hyderabad staff, while continuing his work as a tea server. After much persistence on Sam's part, Baskar attended a DTS in June 1992, and he joined YWAM soon after.

His ministry took him out on the streets of Hyderabad, where painful memories of his own childhood returned as he saw children playing by the roadside, some working at small shops, and others begging. It was impossible for him to detach his emotions and watch the children as an ordinary pedestrian might. He saw beyond their tough demeanor, and connected with their inner turmoil and desperate search for love. Baskar had found hope for his life, and he wanted to give these children that same hope.

Baskar felt called to open a shelter and give these children an opportunity to live off the streets. As Baskar had little finances of his own, trusting God for money to buy a building was a risky adventure. "Surely God is my help; the Lord is the one who sustains me" (Isaiah 45:5) was a verse Baskar turned to for strength as he began this faith journey. Sure enough, the money came in as well as staff to assist in the work. Since the shelter opened, Baskar has daily poured his life into the children, giving them everything he has to offer. Children both on and off the streets have felt his compassion, and through his leadership many are finding a way out of poverty and rejection. Baskar's enthusiasm for God's Word is contagious, and the children learn to share God's love with other street children. Baskar and his wife Marta still live in Hyderabad, where they and their staff have successfully reunited more than 70 street children with their parents.

---

# Jiggu - Reaching An Overlooked Population

Christianity has a long history in South India, and today it still has the highest density of Christians in the country. But within this region is Karnataka, an unreached state with a Christian population of just 1.75%. Because of its location, it is often overlooked in evangelistic efforts, which often focus on the North where there is a greater density of Hindus and Muslims. For this reason, YWAM Bangalore has made it its goal to present Jesus' love in a creative way and raise up strong Kannada (from Karnataka) Christian leaders. In 1996, Jiggu, from Hyderabad, (whose story was told in chapter eight) took up leadership of the YWAM Bangalore base with a cash asset of Rs. 3,500 and 20 staff members. Today the base has multiplied its assets thousands of times over, has 63 staff, and conducts DTS in Kannada (the local language).

In 1996, the YWAM Bangalore staff came together to seek God's next step for them. Normal activities ceased as they focused fully on the Lord. From this prayer time came many new ministries, including one to the children of the Bangalore slums.

The ministry began as many YWAM outreaches do — a cross-cultural team went to a slum, found a public gathering place and attracted crowds with skits, songs and preaching. People came, listened, and then returned to their homes. Each time they went, it was the same story. No heart connection was made with the people. After a few visits, they knew their tactics would have to change if any lasting impact was to be made.

The team returned to prayer and felt they were to clean up the slum. The streets were dirty and sections were filled with human waste. For the slum, there was one public toilet, and this was so filled with waste that the door barely opened. The public toilet had now become the surrounding grounds.

When the YWAM team returned with their brooms and started cleaning up the mess, they quickly drew a crowd of stunned and amused people. Some openly mocked them. Others were shocked that a group of educated, non-slum dwellers would do such a menial task. Yet another set of people told the mockers to be quiet. This group went to their houses, brought their own brooms and helped to clean up their streets.

The cleanup of the slum accomplished what the team couldn't with their skits and songs. This act of servanthood had opened up the hearts of the slum-dwellers to trust them. When the team returned, they were welcomed warmly. Three booths were set up. One which was a beauty salon where children could get their hair and nails cut and cleaned. Another booth was staffed by primary health care workers, giving medical attention where needed. The third booth was for all those desiring prayer.

Lines soon formed outside the booths, so much that they became rowdy as people tried to push their way to the front. A Muslim man kept the crowd in line with the cane wielded in his hand.

Not long after the booths were set up, the team held weekend camps for the children. Including an elder from the community, the children were invited to stay at the YWAM property from Friday to Sunday. They heard Bible studies, received new clothes, and many of them accepted Jesus as their personal Savior. This time was like a mini-DTS for them. There was a definite change in them, both outside and inside, and their relatives often remarked on this. One of the women would tell other slum dwellers, "You should have seen what they did to our kids. If you didn't send your kids you missed an opportunity." In the beginning, around five to ten children came for the weekend. Now there are 200 children.

At the Primary Health Care booth, there have been many miraculous healings and many of those who experienced them are non-believers. A Muslim man came to request treatment for his son. His boy had been taken to several hospitals but no doctors could cure him. The YWAM workers agreed to examine his son, and part of their "diagnostic process" was also to pray with the patients. As they prayed, the son was healed. The father rushed to Jiggu to express his thankfulness. Jiggu smiled, knowing that his medical workers were not full-fledged doctors. "This is not because we are specialized people," said Jiggu. "It's because we believe in God and God uses us." The Muslim man replied, "Sir, 50% medicine and 50% prayer brought healing to my child. I am just happy my son is healed." A seed had been planted in his heart and for many others because their practical and physical needs were met.

One girl who was a regular attendee at the weekend children's camp recently attended a DTS and plans to return as a full-time Mercy Ministry [described on page 168] staff. Other children from these camps are now teenagers and have joyfully pitched in their share as volunteers. The ministry has now evolved to see slum children reaching other slum children.

Jiggu and his team are reaching out to Bangalore in many other ways, including  an outreach to prostitutes, and medical and vocational training. They have also started a radical outreach toward the youth of Bangalore. Within the last few years, Bangalore has emerged as the pub city of India. YWAM has tapped into this trend, opening venues such as a coffeehouse and a Sunday night service specifically orientated toward young people-those most drawn toward this pub culture.

YWAM Bangalore is completely Indian-led and the staff has seen God's faithfulness in paying rental bills, buying new property, and providing protection from those who were hostile with them and took physical action.

# Wilson - Serving the Rejected Ones

"Rejected but Accepted" — These words flashed like neon lights across J.D. Wilson Prabhu's mind as he lay on his bed one evening. This vision, along with two other situations placed in front of him by God, had convinced Wilson of the call upon his life to work with those affected by the HIV/AIDS virus. They were people rejected by society, but accepted by God.

Wilson's first real exposure to the HIV/AIDS problem was in 1993 when he watched a video documenting the AIDS crisis in Africa. In the video children were shown burying their own parents who had died from the disease. After watching this Wilson prayed that he would never be called into this type of work. But God slowly began working on his heart. Two years later he did a DTS in Chennai and began serving on YWAM's church planting team there.

When Wilson received the vision, he knew God was speaking to him. Although he was still reluctant to work in HIV/AIDS ministry, he obediently traveled to Mumbai to receive training from a Christian non-government agency (NGO). It was here that he had his first contact with an AIDS patient and had to confront his fears. Wilson had thought that if he touched or even worked with an HIV/AIDS victim, he too would get the disease. God showed him this was not true.

While in Mumbai, Wilson's trainer asked him to pray for one of the patients. Putting aside his own fears he laid his hands on the patient and prayed for him. From that moment, Wilson's fears left him, and God began to impart His compassion to Wilson for these people. During those six weeks of training, Wilson spent time with each patient, eating with them, drinking tea with them, and sometimes just listening to them. He discovered they were really just ordinary people, and he wasn't going to catch the virus from them. They shared many of the same basic desires as he did. The only difference was they were sick and robbed of their joy and often their dignity.

With the training over, Wilson returned to Chennai with a fire burning in his own heart. He had dreams of starting a ministry, reaching out to HIV/AIDS victims and restoring their joy and dignity in life. For two months, he met with various NGOs, finding out what they were doing about HIV/AIDS. Many were involved in education and spreading awareness about the disease, but none were providing any personal care for AIDS victims. Here was a perfect opportunity for YWAM to fill a need by providing a hospice where patients could spend their final days receiving compassionate care. Wanting to be equipped and fully trained before starting anything,

Wilson volunteered for eight months in an NGO. He then began to volunteer his time at Chennai's Tuberculosis (TB) Sanatorium. During his time there, he recruited workers, and they named their new ministry PACT (Project AIDS through Care and Training)

By this time, the chief doctor at the Sanatorium had opened up two wards for AIDS patients, making it the largest hospital in South Asia for AIDS patients. While Wilson was there, he was dismayed to see patients being turned away to make room for others who had a smaller chance of surviving. Those turned away had no place to go. Their families had rejected them, and they often had to sleep on train platforms or the streets. Women were the most vulnerable. Those who did get hospice treatment were often there for months, and no one ever visited them.

Near to the Sanatorium, an NGO had opened up a hospice in 1998, but it closed due to lack of training and staff. Its leader approached Wilson and his team to take over the hospice. With no source for funding but a clear approval from the Lord, they said yes. The hospice would be for women affected by the virus, because of their greater vulnerability.

Wilson was to take over the hospice leadership in March 2000, but by the month's first week, he still had no funding. In the last week of March, he received an email saying a church wanted to sponsor the hospice and their check would arrive soon. At the end of March, the hospice opened with ten beds.

The hospice has been running for four years now and has treated more than 80 women patients. Some have passed away. Some have been successfully reunited with their families. The reconciliation process isn't always easy. The team from the hospice sits down with each family, explaining to them every step of the disease, dispelling any myths. Sometimes the process takes only a few months, for other families it can take over a year. The team continues working with the family for six months after the reconciliation takes place.

Other NGOs around Chennai have opened up hospices, but PACT continues to receive the most calls. The reason is their emphasis on personal care. The patients at the hospice are treated as people, not just patients.

PACT also has a children's hospice for children who are HIV positive. These children receive education, medical care, moral care and support. They have just recently opened up a separate hospice for them. Their dream for the children's hospice is to establish "family groups", delegating a couple over a group of children so they can receive the love and care of "parents". PACT would like to see more hospices throughout India, and they are already helping train YWAM staff to start similar ministries in their own cities. The training is conducted through apprenticeships, under the authority of experienced caregivers or social workers. Since its beginnings, PACT has counseled and met the needs of around 15,000 HIV patients.

# A Rambo in Andhra Pradesh

Victor Kathramalla watched in rapt attention as movie superhero Rambo battled the forces of evil. After the film's closing scene, the credits scrolled down the screen, but Victor kept staring at the screen. He thought, *Rambo had a mission, what is my mission?*

Victor kept searching for the answer to that question and a few months later it led him to give his life to the Lord. As a young Christian, he began to wonder how he could serve the Lord. A friend asked him if he had heard of Youth With A Mission. He immediately thought of the Rambo movie. *This can be my mission. I can be a Rambo for Christ.*

At the same time, God had been continually leading him toward Luke 9:23, "If anyone would come after me, he must deny himself and take up his cross daily and follow me."

In April 1987, Victor and his friends invited a YWAM team to perform at their church's youth gathering. After their skits and songs, the team leader shared from Luke 9:23. Victor wanted to follow Christ whole-heartedly, but didn't understand what it meant to deny himself and daily take up his cross. From all he had heard these visitors say about DTS, he sensed this was the place where he would gain this understanding.

Victor attended DTS in Chennai that summer and discovered that God had a call on his life to help complete the Great Commission. He remained in Chennai for two more years, serving as DTS staff. Near the end of this time, he heard about a School of Biblical Studies (SBS) starting in Goa. He intended to attend it, but since there were two months until it began, Victor went to spend one month with YWAM Hyderabad. A visiting speaker from Sri Lanka just happened to be there at the time, and he imparted some wisdom to Victor that forever changed his life. He said, "If you really want God to release you into your own vision, you must prove faithful in serving someone else's vision, like Joshua faithfully served Moses' vision before he was released into his own ministry." He suggested that Victor serve Sam Dharam's vision for the next two years. (Sam was the Hyderabad base leader at the time.)

These words didn't fit into Victor's plan, and he mentioned to the speaker about the upcoming SBS in Goa. The speaker asked if he had really sought God's approval for it. Victor prayerfully considered the issue, also asking Sam to seek God's answer about the SBS. Within a week, both had heard a clear no. Victor knew what the next step was. He committed to serve Sam's vision for two years. Sam gratefully accepted and assigned him to be the base accountant, a job Victor wasn't enthusiastic about.

However, this Sri Lankan's impact on Victor wasn't over yet. He told him a story about two Christian workers who ministered in two different regions each with approximately 100 villages under similar conditions. One itinerant worker preached in all of the 100 villages in the space of one year. The other worker came to the second region and only concentrated his efforts on one village. Here he planted a church and raised up 15 strong disciples in the span of a year. After the year was over, they returned to their homes. Ten years later they both returned to see the fruit of their labor. The people whom the itinerant Christian worker won to the Lord had returned to their old ways. The people whom the second worker had made contact with were still strong in their faith and were spreading the gospel.

Another thing that convinced Victor of the need for discipleship was a conversation he had with a villager during a DTS outreach. The man said to him, "Tomorrow you leave. All our lives we grew up taking the names of Rama and Krishna when we were in trouble. That just comes to us naturally. Who will teach us to grow in this new faith?"

These two incidents propelled Victor's vision for discipleship to a whole new level. He knew there were many in India who could not afford to attend DTS. So the Lord showed how to disciple people in the local church. Victor's plan was to plant churches in such a manner that they would multiply themselves, and the main focus would be to disciple Christians. He shared this with Sam, who in turn suggested he write up a proposal and submit it to YWAM India's National Council. In January 1994, he moved to Vishakapatnam with his wife, Sarojini, their daughter and two men to start this ministry, REAP (Reach Entire Andhra Pradesh).

The REAP team traveled to villages scattered throughout Andhra Pradesh, remaining in one village for two years. At the end of those two years, their plan was to see at least two people discipled and equipped to carry on the work. Planting churches was a secondary goal. When REAP enters a village, their plan is to improve the economical, psychological, physical, and spiritual life of the village. The initial stages of the work involve entering a village and inquiring after people's daily needs, such as milk, water, and livestock. This builds trust with the villagers. In a village where a people called the Yerukalas resided, REAP transcended borders in a way no other evangelism groups had before.

The Yerukalas are a group of Tamils who fled their state many years ago. They were formerly roadside robbers, but now sell *arak* (cheap liquor) to make a living. Because of their association with pigs they are treated as the least amongst the *Untouchables*. When REAP entered this village, the Yerukalas offered them water as a polite gesture but really expected refusal. When the team accepted and also drank the water, the villagers were shocked. When offered a meal, REAP also accepted. The Yerukalas wondered what type of people would accept water and food from people such as themselves. Other Christians had entered their village, but would not drink water from them or reside with them. With their hearts opened, the villagers welcomed the REAP team, saying, "You can come any day, any time and stay with us. You come and tell us about Jesus. We have heard about Jesus, they have come and preached, but they always stay away. They preach Jesus' love and then walk away." Today, REAP has seen more than 90 people profess a faith in Jesus from this village. The villagers are enthusiastic about REAP going to other villages where their relatives live.

Like Rambo, Victor found his mission and through REAP he has passed it on to many others eager to see discipleship in close partnership with evangelism. Victor looks back on those two years in Hyderabad as crucial time of personal formation. It was a time of God teaching him the value of faithfully serving the vision of another. If he had gone on to SBS, he might have never learnt this lesson and might never have met his wife Sarojini, who was on staff in Hyderabad at the time. In order to realize his dreams, first Victor had to lay down his desires. God has honored that sacrifice. Today there are 26 people working with REAP, 650 believers within the 32 churches and 25 Bible study groups planted by REAP. This ministry has brought the teaching of DTS to people who otherwise could not attend.

Today Victor and Sarojini and their three children reside in Hyderabad. Victor has been serving as the Director of YWAM South India for the last seven years, and in 2003 took on the role of National Chairman for YWAM India while still working with REAP.

---

# An Internet Café
# with a Difference in Indore

Ministry has started to come out of its traditional mould. The evangelistic practice of standing on the streets, passing out tracts, performing skits and dances, and talking to people afterward does not apply everywhere. It is not a form readily accepted within an urban context. Ministry forms now have been contextualized into different cultural forms and lifestyles, with which people can identify.

Since its beginnings in 1999, YWAM Indore has grown into a multi-faceted centre reaching out to various people groups. One of their targeted groups is the internet culture. In any city in India, there are an abundance of internet cafes. Although the number of personal computers to a home is increasing, there still remain a great number of homes without computers and access to the World Wide Web.

YWAM Indore opened an internet café that looks like any other café. It has 10 internet-accessible computers and the usual coffees and teas. What sets their café apart is its staff. They are friendly and helpful because their focus goes beyond mere transactions. They seek to build deeper relationships with their customers. YWAM Indore's internet café is a bridge to friendship evangelism. They have taken the regular customers out on picnics and social events. And it is here that they have had a chance to share the love of Jesus with them.

This internet café is one of the many ministries Ramchand Saranu had a vision to see started in Indore. Ramchand, the leader of the YWAM Indore base, is a South Indian himself, an outsider to this community. But he says he has faced no hindrances because of his origin. There are many North Indians involved in the base, and Ramchand continues to search for new ways of reaching out to the people of Indore. One of his plans for the future is to start small businesses. In recent years, he has struck up friendships with business men. They have everything money can buy, but are lacking the one thing that really carries meaning in life. He wants to help them find Jesus, but to bridge a natural social division, he recognizes that he and other Christians must approach them on their own level – as business men. Therefore, Ramchand is exploring ways to start a business so as to open doors for evangelism into the business community.

Ramchand is involved in strategizing new ways to reach every sector of Indore's society. He also plans to move into the Muslim community, to fellowship with them, and share with them the good news he has found in his own life. Muslim's make up 16% of

Indore's three million population. What Ramchand is doing in India is a small representation of the changing methods of evangelism taking place throughout YWAM South Asia.

# Giving Back What She Was Once Deprived Of

"For I know the plans I have for you," declares the Lord, "plans to prosper you and not to harm you, plans to give you hope and a future" (Jeremiah 29:11). Eight-year-old Anupama Dongardive read this, delighted and strengthened in the verse she knew God had given her. Anupama (Anu) had just recently committed her life to the Lord.

Since the age of 10 months, she had been living in Pandita Ramabai Mukti Mission as an orphan. When she reached school age, she was placed in a convent school. Because she was an orphan, her classmates were not keen to become her friends. Throughout her years here, she faced much rejection and grew up with little love.

Eight-year-old Anu held desperately onto the hope in Jeremiah 29:11. She had heard the Lord clearly say that one day she would be a mother to many children. Although she did not fully understand what this meant, from that point on, Anu's heart was filled with compassion for others in a similar state of neglect or abandonment. As Anu grew older, these thoughts grew and birthed the idea for Vanitashray (home for girls).

Vanitashray takes in girls who are either orphans or have been abandoned by their parents. In 2001, the first girl to live in Anu's home arrived. When she first saw the girl, Nikita, she appeared to be only eight months old. Anu was shocked to find out that Nikita was actually 3 years old. In the three months before her arrival, Nikita's father had slipped deeper into alcoholic addiction. With no desire to properly take care of his daughter, he put her to sleep each night with a sleeping pill, and stopped feeding her and had plans to sell her for Rs. 2000. An NGO heard of her plight and brought her 150 kilometers to Pune. Vanitashray was just starting in Pune, and this particular NGO believed it was the best place for little Nikita.

"It took her a year to begin speaking and walking, because of the trauma she had been through," Anu remembered. "She would just sit and stare at us. Her father came to visit her a couple times, but she never recognized him. Today she can sing and pray, she is a very intellectual girl."

News about Vanitashray spread and more girls were referred to her. Today, Anu has rented a flat next to her own in which live 15 girls. There are three full-time caretakers who provide for the girl's needs.

Anu's desire to start such a place was so strong that not even a tragedy deterred her. Her husband, Silas, shared Anu's compassion for orphans and had plans to work alongside her. Yet in 2001, the same year Vanitashray started, Silas suffered a heart attack and died. Despite the tremendous grief in her own heart, she knew Vanitashray had to continue, and it did.

It is the memory of her past that fuels Anu's work. "I grew up in the orphanage and missed out being loved and accepted. I do not want these girls to miss out on that," Anu says. Her dreams for her two daughters are the same as for these precious girls; that they would grow up to be independent women with a freedom from the rejection which haunted Anu throughout her childhood.

Anu does not want these "homes" to become larger, because then the girls would miss out on the love and care they so need. Rather, she has a vision to see several "homes" open in Pune, each built around this simple principle. While at the moment, all the staff are female, Anu would like to see each "home" run by a couple, as she fully understands the importance of the girls having father figure in their lives.

Vanitashray is a part of YWAM Pune's ministry. Anu did her DTS in 1991 in Pune. Besides giving her time to the girls of Vanitashray, she is also YWAM Pune's City Co-coordinator.

# EPILOGUE

*I*n 1994, I left Chennai to attend a boarding school 12 hours away. After five years there, I left for America to attend university. During my brief visits home, I attended YWAM gatherings and parties, eager to catch up with "family." Each time I attended these gatherings, I recognized fewer and fewer familiar faces. Many faces smiled at me knowingly. I had no idea who they were, but they knew me. I was Tim and Karol Svoboda's daughter home in Chennai for the holidays.

Each time I returned, YWAM Chennai had grown. I knew it wasn't only Chennai that was like this; it was all of YWAM South Asia. If I were to attend a regional conference, my feelings of being lost would be amplified, with 1,425 staff in all of South Asia.

Since that GO Fest in Mumbai in 1988, YWAM South Asia has gone through many changes. The demographics have shifted to a majority of national workers, and the population involves a healthy mixture of young people as well as those in their "mature" years. Besides structural changes, there have been several marriages of YWAM South Asia pioneers. In 1989, Steve Cochrane and Elisabeth Baumann were married. Still pioneers at heart, they prayed together about where to live, and felt they were to move to Pune, where Elisabeth pioneered the base and Steve pioneered Frontier

Missions in the country.

In 1989, Wendy Mahbert married David Paul in Darjeeling. I still have fond memories of my sister Ana and I being Wendy's flower girls. David and Wendy worked for many years in Delhi, helping establish a YWAM base there.

Brad and Debbie Carr came into YWAM as singles and were married in 1985. Together, they helped pioneer the Kolkata base and lived there for many years. They now are based in Chennai where they are sending out teams to new frontiers.

After Sandra completed her DTS, fellow YWAMer Ian Liu proposed to her. Leaders had approached both of them, suggesting the other for a lifetime mate. Sandra initially brushed it off, only seeing Ian as a good friend from her church in Kolkata. But her mind obviously changed because she said yes to his proposal. They were married in 1988.

Richie and Cheryl Kleinman both did their DTS in Chennai, but as singles. Both were from Kolkata and knew each other before. After their wedding in 1986, they settled down in Chennai where they have been serving ever since.

In 1990, Leaula Aufai married Corina Alexander. Corina had been the first Bangladeshi student at the Uluberia DTS, and it was her family that offered Leaula a place to stay when he first arrived in Bangladesh. Together they have been a part of the ongoing work in Bangladesh.

That sums up the weddings of the YWAM old-timers — or "dinosaurs" as they sometimes call themselves – with their grey hairs, balding areas and wrinkles showing up.

There is so much interconnectivity that YWAM South Asia sometimes feels like one "work". Leaders help one another through their network of contacts, and there is a constant effort to stay in touch and encourage each other. This foundation of relationships has remained as YWAM has expanded beyond everyone's dreams. The work in each country today carries its own stories – stories of both despair and triumph. In closing I want to lay out a brief progress report of YWAM in each country. Each is a unique work of God and all glory goes to Him for their success.

# India

At the beginning, YWAM India was around 70% foreign and 30% Indian in its staff and was viewed as an expatriate agency. When my father became the National Director in 1989, the Indian to foreign ratio was at 60-40%, and quickly changing. His goal was to change the ratio to a majority of national staff, and through policies he wrote, the ratio is now 76% Indian to 24% foreign.

In 1996, Sam Dharam from Hyderabad became the National Director. His leadership brought much-needed change during a period of explosive growth. Sam saw that central leadership was no longer suitable to the direction of YWAM India. To effectively minister to India's diversity, Sam split YWAM India into five zones, with a leader placed over each one. This change released YWAM workers to fast-forward their dreams for India to reality. Growth exploded across the nation. Empowered by this new way of functioning, leaders rose up from the grassroots level.

After many years of dreaming, YWAM's University of the Nations in India finally has its own campus located on a beautiful property in Lonavala (between Pune and Mumbai). In June 2004, they began their first quarter (term) with four schools and 50 students and are moving toward a goal of 134 students a quarter.

From their simple beginnings in a Kolkata guesthouse, YWAM India now has over 1,100 workers. Some 10,000 students have passed through its DTSes. As an organization, it has gained respect. First viewed with cynicism because of its youthfulness, pastors now seek YWAM India's voice.

Not only is YWAM India impacting those within its borders, but those outside its borders as well. Brad Carr, who came in November 1982 and worked alongside Steve Cochrane in Kolkata, is today based in Chennai. Along with his wife, Debbie, they are leading the School of Evangelism and Pioneering (SOEP), imparting to others the lessons they learned during their pioneering years. Out of the SOEP, India sent out its first team to start YWAM in a new and unfamiliar country. It began with one Indian student who approached Brad and shared his burden for Africa. Pulling together a team, this young man led them to Sierra Leone in 1995. They left a few months later due to a political crisis, but relocated to The Gambia, where they now work in a Muslim village. This was the first Indian team to leave India to launch a new YWAM centre. Since then, Indian pioneers have been sent to Guyana, (South America), China, Laos and Bhutan. And there are plans to go to many more countries.

# Nepal

Most of the foreign workers who pioneered YWAM in this mostly Hindu kingdom have moved on to other areas of Asia. But their prayers, service and sensitivity drew Nepali nationals to join the mission. Among them are Kishor, Moti and Sukadev, who remain in Nepal today. YWAM Nepal continues to grow in size and strength. First established in Kathmandu, YWAM's work was pioneered into many rural areas after 1992 by Nepalis, Indians and foreigners alike. Today, there are 180 staff working in 18 different locations.

Kishor Rana has had a significant role in this growth. He first met James and Jean Smith through the Bible studies they had in their home. Reading his Bible one day, he came across the verse in Isaiah 52 that says, "How beautiful on the mountain are the feet of those who bring good news." The verse reminded him of Nepal's renowned Himalayan mountain ranges. He thought, "Nepal has mountains. I can bring the good news to my country." This was the start of his adventure with YWAM Nepal.

Kishor's heart has been to implement more training to equip workers to bring the Good News throughout the mountains and valleys of Nepal. In the pioneering days, James was sometimes unable to lead because of severe sickness. In those times Kishor stepped in to help. At the time it seemed coincidence, but in hindsight it was a time of sharpening Kishor's leadership skills. In 1999, he became the National Director of Nepal and still leads the work there today. Besides faithfully persevering in his own country, he is sending out teams to countries outside of Nepal's borders.

Although the work in Nepal has sometimes struggled, a YWAM-sponsored prayer walk has given a tremendous boost to Kishor and other Christian leaders in the nation. On January 1, 2000 – after a night of praying and fasting – hundreds of people set out from the far eastern corner of Nepal. Their goal was to walk 250 kilometers until another group would take over. That group would carry on until the fourth (and last) group reached the western corner of Nepal.

YWAM Nepal organized this event, *Bless Nepal 2000*, in full collaboration with churches and Christian organizations in Nepal. It was the first-ever high profile Christian event held in Nepal. During the organization phase, many expressed doubts that the walkers would successfully make it to the second zone due to security measures.

The walkers were stopped by the police as they reached the second zone and were questioned about what they were doing. The walkers shared their reasons, not hiding the fact that this was a religious event. The only objection the police raised was that the group was not carrying a banner. The group joyfully procured a banner with the words "Bless Nepal 2000" on it and continued their walk.

As they stopped in villages along the way, each group conducted health camps, held cultural events, performed skits and did community service work such as sweeping market places. *Bless Nepal 2000* took a month to complete and covered 900kms of Nepal. The Christian community was stunned by its success. The event was intended to unite the Nepali churches in prayer and missions, and the walk showed them what was really possible. In all, over 1,000 Nepalis participated in this walk. Its success went beyond what many Christians believed was possible in Nepal.

For those involved in YWAM, the staff saw that even they could be used by God to lead a nation-wide event. God's blessing had truly been on them, and it was His blessing that brought *Bless Nepal 2000's* success. God's blessing has been in YWAM Nepal since its birth, and was most evident with this event!

# Bangladesh

In 1986, after Leaula Aufai had faithfully worked solo in Bangladesh for a year, four people joined him. Leaula's heart for Bangladesh from the very beginning was to plant churches and to involve Bengalis in this work with him. He knew it was important to have DTSes, to train Bengalis for the work. Yet by 1990, none on the team in Bangladesh had a desire to begin DTSes, and there didn't seem to be anyone coming from outside. Leaula carried on with his work, hoping the right person would arrive. Then God said to him, "Leaula, what you are doing is great, but you need to multiply yourself." Setting aside for a time his desires for pioneering and church planting, Leaula began the first DTS in 1990 in Dhaka, Bangladesh, with 11 students. Since then, Bangladesh has had a steady growth. As of 2004, it has a task force of 100 staff to meet the felt needs of the Bengali people.

It has been a struggle for Bengalis to join YWAM. Many of those who join the mission are first-generation Christians and do not have the support of their families. Also because of the Muslim background of the country, converting to Christianity can cause a person to be rejected by their family. Regardless, many of the Bengali workers have remained, serving others not for their own benefit but for the Glory of God.

Today, YWAM Bangladesh works in five major cities of the country. There is a vision to send Bengalis into other countries as missionaries. Although not a reality yet, it is a dream pressing heavily on the heart of YWAM Bangladesh staff. Their areas of focus are Central Asia and the Middle East.

# Sri Lanka

In 1992, a couple gave up their successful business in South Korea to pioneer YWAM in Sri Lanka. They started their work in a small hill town. Their vision for YWAM's work in the country is to equip and train Christian disciples. Since 1992, 13 DTSes have

been run through which 300 Sri Lankans have attended. YWAM
is now located in two towns. Their ministries have expanded into
King's Kids (ministering to children); giving practical help in the
area of medicine; providing shelter for those without; and working
alongside the Sri Lankan churches.

The country of Bhutan has been on the hearts of many in
YWAM South Asia for several years. Since 1985, short-term teams
have gone into this country, the only Tibetan Buddhist Kingdom
in the world. But when a team of six YWAMers set about to pioneer
a work there in February 2004, it was a jubilant celebration as a
long-held dream was fulfilled. In 1984, James Smith had a vision
of lights reaching out of Nepal into the Himalayan world, one of
these countries being Bhutan. Some of those who were involved
with YWAM Nepal are now the very ones involved in the pioneering
of YWAM Bhutan.

The road ahead is laden with surprises and developments
for YWAM South Asia. When I traveled around India and Nepal
interviewing people for this book, one of the questions I asked was
"What direction do you see YWAM South Asia headed in?" Because
of the great leaps the mission has made, this question was answered
with great expectations for the future ahead. Here is what a few of
them had to say.

*I see YWAM's future in South Asia, to quote William Carey,
as "bright as the promises of God". I think there is no reason
other than our own stumbling why we won't have someday
over 50,000 South Asians having gone through DTS, have over
10,000 long term staff, 100,000 churches planted among the*

*unreached, have trained many Christian politicians to take major political roles, have numerous AIDS ministries, widow's homes and orphanages.*

~ Steve Cochrane

*I think YWAM's got a tremendous future. We have great leaders and great committed staff. What I'd like to see is YWAM in every state in India. We're almost there actually. We'd like to see 5,000 YWAMers by 2010.*

*If you ask me what my dream is for India, it is that I would like to see us in 120 cities and 500 villages. Geographically, primarily to start some aspect of ministry that has an impact on society. When God looks at ministry, He doesn't look at political borders. He looks at people. So when we are persuaded to a different kind of a passion toward a particular ministry, then we don't see borders, we just see people where that ministry is going to be effectively employed and benefited for the people. We just see people and we go there to do it.*

~ Sam Dharam,

*Nepal is called to go to every part of the world. Already we had three teams go to Myanmar. We just had a team that came back two weeks ago from Malaysia. I took a team to Kenya and Ethiopia, and there's a very strong call for YWAM Nepal to send missionaries out to other parts of the world. I believe that's their destiny, part of their heritage. It's what God is going to do. They're going to continue to expand. It's really a work of the Holy Spirit that is not contingent on what person is there.*

~ James Smith

*I think YWAM India is getting ready for mass urbanization. There will be a lot of Indians involved, leading different kinds of ministries. That's where the next 10-20 years is going to be. India is changing really rapidly. It's becoming urbanized. YWAM is one of the few organizations on the cutting edge of the urbanization process taking place in India. Because of what is happening in India, YWAM will play a major role in spearheading the urbanization in India.*

~ Wilfred Selvaraj (YWAM Chennai)

*We are now more planted, more established. We have more properties, facilities, schools and assets. There is the potential of YWAM becoming a wealthy organization. But we will continue to be cutting edge because YWAM isn't afraid to try new things. I think we will continue to expand into different parts of India. There is still so much of the nation that we aren't in. There are still so many people who don't know Jesus.*

~ Brad Carr *(Chennai SOEP leader)*

YWAM's greatest asset has been its flexibility; this is what has carried it into the millennium, making it relevant to its environment. It has moved beyond the traditional evangelism form of open-airs and adapted to more relevant forms. These include YWAM Bangalore's Youth Centre, internet cafés, shelters for street children and hospices for those affected by the HIV/AIDS virus. Teams also minister to lepers, slum dwellers, and working parents (providing child day-care). These ministries have come to signify evangelism as a way of living out Jesus' love by example. Open-airs are still effective, but YWAM's flexibility has led to a greater diversity of ministries.

I would like to close with an excerpt from a letter my mother had written to our friends and family. She tells of her vision for YWAM. The letter is dated November 11, 1987. Even though written 19 years ago, it still has relevancy to YWAM South Asia today.

*We want to share a few thoughts with you on what the Lord has been doing in our midst lately. Psalm 133 clearly tells us of the beauty of unity and the blessing that comes with it. We've had some very precious times recently of sharing our hearts and expressing our loving commitment to one another in our YWAM community. From that, we've become more deeply aware of the love that God wants between us. A love that forgives, is vulnerable, gently corrects, lays down rights for the other person and empathizes with others. Loving, godly relationships are our example to the world of God's love. Therefore, it is the first thing that Satan wants to destroy between us. We see it all around us and perhaps in our own lives. It's something we need to work diligently at, so that we can destroy the works of the devil. We're praying that God will continue to deepen and grow our love, so that we can freely show the world His love.*

These words show the core reason why so many people were willing to leave their homes to pioneer YWAM. They came because of the love for these nations. They were enabled to stay, firstly because of God's love, and secondly because of loving relationships they developed. With these came a fierce determination to remain. YWAM International's motto is *To Know God and To Make Him Known*. This is the heart cry of YWAM South Asia for the countries of India, Nepal, Bangladesh, Sri Lanka, Bhutan and beyond, so that they will see the light of God shining through. This heart cry remains in their footsteps of faith imprinted across South Asia.

# Notes

[1] *salwar* : An Indian outfit worn by a woman. It is a knee length dress worn with baggy pants.

[2] *garam chai* : Hot tea

[3] *misti dhoi* : Sweetened yoghurt

[4] *Uluberia* is one hour south of Kolkata

[5] Today *Ragha* is serving the Lord in Japan. In 1989, Ragha left India to the bittersweet rejoicing of his brothers and sisters here. It was a sad send-off because they were losing an Indian brother, but it was also a joyous one as Ragha was the first Indian missionary to be sent out of YWAM India. Today Ragha is happily married  to Akemi, from Japan and they have one daughter. Ragha and Akemi are both involved in church planting.

[6] Zechariah 4:10

[7] *tariq* : A paper to verify the accused had not left the country.

[8] *Flock group* is the old term for the small groups formed in DTS.

[9] *pyjama kurta* : Men's clothing-baggy pants and long shirt

[10] *churidar* : Women's clothing-dress with trousers.

[11] *dosai* : Thin crepe-like item made out of rice flour and lentils.

[12] *chapatti* : Flat bread roasted over a fire.

[13] *dosai* : dosai with a potato filling.

[14] Story in Chapter 4. The arrest happened in March 1985.

[15] *roti* : Flat bread roasted over a fire.

[16] *paise* : Coins, 100 paise=1 Rupee

[17] *puri* : Deep-fried bread

[17] *taka* : Bangladesh currency

[19] *goja* : A sweet

[20] The *Injil* is the New Testament and 'required' reading for Muslims. However Muslims have rejected it saying it has been changed and therefore not worth reading.

[21] *Pandita Ramabai,* born in Western Maharashtra, was a champion for women's causes in India, advocating for the education of women. She died in 1922.

[22] *shamiyana* : A large covering, often brightly colored, under which outdoor gatherings take place.

[23] *sherpa* : Nepali trekking guides

# WHAT IS YWAM ?

Youth With A Mission began its work in India in 1982 by establishing its first training center in the city of Kolkata. Today in the Subcontinent YWAM has over 1200 staff in over 160 locations. The work of YWAM is in three major areas: Training, Mercy Ministries, and Evangelism.

Youth With A Mission offers many training programs that can lead to a Bachelor's or Master's Degree in their worldwide University of the Nations. The entrance course is the Discipleship Training School which is offered in India in Tamil, English, Hindi, Bengali, Telugu, Marathi, Nepali, and is starting in other languages as well. This 6 month training course includes topics like Holiness, Worship, Intercession, Inner Healing, How to Hear the Voice of God, Evangelism, Victory over Sin and much more. Topics are not only taught and discussed but modeled and applied into the student's life. After the Discipleship Training School there are many other courses one can apply for. The Discipleship Training School is the entrance course into YWAM which has 7 colleges. Those colleges are:

> The College of Christian Ministries
> The College of Science and Technology
> The College of Humanities and International Studies
> The College of The Arts
> The College of Counseling and Health Care
> The College of Education
> The College of Communication

In each of these colleges there are many courses which prepare the student not only for full time ministry but for ministry in the secular world as they serve in their job sharing God's heart with scientists, business people, lawyers, doctors, and other professionals who may be beyond the reach of the full time minister.

## ~ Mercy Ministries ~

"When Jesus landed and SAW a large crowd, He had Compassion on them and he HEALED their sick." Matthew 14:14.

Through the simplicity of this verse we gain insight into the heart of mercy. Jesus SAW the people. He was not ignorant of disease, poverty, or problems. Secondly, He had COMPASSION on the people. Their hurts became His hurts and he identified with their pain. He was motivated to take action and he healed them. Jesus knew what was wrong and what He needed to do for the people.

YWAM Mercy ministries are now active all over the country of India. There are many slum projects in the inner cities where we are helping people through primary health care, literacy training, day care centers and community development. In other areas of the nation YWAM is conducting drug rehabilitation programs, working amongst the street children, ministering to HIV / AIDS infected people, suicide counseling, leprosy relief projects and meeting the needs of those that are suffering in practical ways.

## ~ Evangelism ~

YWAM has many creative methods of making God known to people. Coffee houses, building friendships, in the villages, on the streets, and in many different ways. YWAM endeavors to share God's love with people through the message of the gospel so that God and His ways might be known to all people.

## How Do You Join YWAM?

All those that want to join YWAM need to complete a six-month Discipleship Training School. The Discipleship Training School is offered in both Tamil and English in the city of Chennai. For more information please write to:

Youth With A Mission
P.O. Box. 1301
St. Thomas Mount
Chennai, Tamil Nadu
India 600 016.

# BOOKS AVAILABLE
## FROM
# YWAM PUBLISHING PVT. LTD.

**Is That Really You God?**                                   Rs. 80
by *Loren Cunningham*

[Tamil Edition]                                              Rs. 50

Is That Really You, God? is not only a practical guide to hearing God's voice but also an amazing testimony to how following His direction can impact our lives and the world for the glory of God's kingdom. The story of YWAM has much to teach us about listening to God as we seek to be used by Him. [PAGES 187]

**Making Jesus Lord**                                        Rs. 85
by *Loren Cunningham*

We live in a world where the exultation of rights has become an obsession. Because personal rights do hold great value, we can perform no greater act of faith and worship than to consciously lay down these rights at the feet of the One who has gone before us! Loren Cunningham details proven steps to a life of freedom, joy, and intimate fellowship with God. [PAGES 152]

**Daring to Live on the Edge**                               Rs. 99
by *Loren Cunningham*

Living by faith is not the domain of only those Christians called to "full-time" ministry. Every Christian can enter into the adventure. What is important is not our vocation, but whether we are committed to obeying God's will in our lives. If you are willing to step out in faith and trust in God, doing whatever it is He has asked you to do, then you will see His provision. Once you have experienced this, you will be spoiled for the ordinary. [PAGES 206]

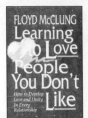

### Learning to Love People You Don't Like    Rs. 60
by *Floyd McClung*

Biblical unity is attainable! Floyd McClung Jr. offers challenging and practical answers for achieving productive, lasting relationships. Here is a first-hand account of how anyone can live in love and unity with others, both in the church and in the world. [PAGES 116]

### Imprisoned in Iran    Rs. 110
by *Dan Baumann*

Wrongly accused of espionage and thrown into the most infamous high security prison in Iran, Dan Baumann witnessed the powerful triumph of God's love over fear. [PAGES 224]

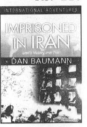

### Transformation 1 VCD    Rs. 125
[in Hindi, English, or Tamil]

This is an exciting video presentation of 4 cities from different countries and how they were transformed when pastors and Christians from across denominations gathered together for united prayer and worship. Crime, drugs, suicide, murder, and other social problems began to be cleaned up as God came to their cities. Transformation video gives us a clear understanding of what God expects from us if we want to see his visitation come to our cities. This video is now available in English, Hindi, or Tamil.

### Breakthrough    Rs. 60
by *Rudi Lac*

If you want to see God use you to break into new territory for His Kingdom then this is the book for you to read. Rudi shares exciting stories of how God used him in dark and difficult places. It is a book that you cannot put down, as

you want to keep on reading what will happen next. Rudi weaves into the book principles of prayer, intercession, hearing the voice of God, worship, and other spiritual elements that are essential to see God use you to make a breakthrough. [Pages 266]

Rs. 65

Veteran missionary Ross Tooley, who for over thirty years has been personally presenting the gospel, shares on heart to heart evangelism. Tooley examines honest and effective ways of approaching both those close to home and those from more distant cultures and backgrounds. [Pages 223]

## Companion to the Poor
Rs. 99
by *Viv Grigg*

Companion to the Poor projects a vision of what it means to introduce the kingdom of the Lord Jesus among the slum dwellers of an Asian city. Asia's slum people are poor largely because of injustice and oppression. This book is the story of a rich Westerner trying to understand discipleship in the context of such injustice, poverty, and corruption-incidentally, the social context of most of the Scriptures. [Pages 209]

## Beholding the Beauty of God
Rs. 115
by *Greg E. Wiley*

This is a study guide for your devotional life on the character and nature

of God. Greg has put together many scriptures to explain God's Justice, Love, Goodness and many more facets of His character. Greg gives a detailed study on the names of God and the book is full of quotes by A.W. Tozer and other men of God who had a unique walk with the Lord. This is a book that you will use again and again to draw close to the Lord. [Pages 201]

### Ears to Hear
by *Deborah Wiley*

Rs. 85

This is a practical book on how God speaks and how you can learn to listen to the voice of God. Deborah Wiley lives this message. She along with her husband are the national prayer events coordinators for YWAM India. She has done an in-depth study on how God speaks and shares principles that she has tested in her own life. If you have questions on how to hear the voice of God then this book is for you. [PAGES 144]

### Spiritual Warfare
by *Dean Sherman*

Rs. 99

How to Live in Victory and Retake the Land / God has called Christians to overcome the world and drive back the forces of evil and darkness at work within it. Spiritual warfare isn't just casting out demons; it's Spirit-controlled thinking and attitudes. Dean delivers a no-nonsense, both-feet-planted-on-the-ground approach to the unseen world. [PAGES 220]

### The Life Model
Living from the Heart Jesus Gave You

Rs. 99

The Life Model is a unifying approach to ministries of counseling, recovery, pastoral care, deliverance, and inner healing. This book is widely used

by churches, missions, and leaders to help them restore wholeness in the lives of hurting people. Whether you are a church or mission's leader or a person that needs help in restoring your inner person to the wholeness and abundant life that Jesus promises then this is the book for you to read as it gives professional and solid Christian counseling principles for life issues. [162 PAGES]

## Marriage Masala
### by *Rod and Ruthie Gilbert*

Rs. 125

This is a book of 52 spices (one for every week of the year) to give fun and inspiration to any couple in helping them with their marriage. Rod and Ruthie in this manual help to make good marriages healthier.

Rod and Ruthie have 27 years of marriage experience and have brought up 5 children. They have spent the majority of their life here in India and their book is based on the problems and rewards of marriage in the Subcontinent Context. Some of the topics Rod and Ruthie cover are Communication, Dating in your marriage, Boundaries, Authority and Submission, Love Languages, Sex in Marriage, Balancing Marriage and Ministry, how to handle in-laws and much more. The book is full of practical advice, illustrations, and sound teaching. [176 PAGES]